To John Patterson '57
Best wishes
Roger Burke

Y0-ABO-414

$2 —

Once A Husky, Always A Husky

Roger Burke

Columbia River Book Co.,
3404 S. Auburn
Kennewick, Wash 99337

Copyright (c) 2001 Columbia River Book Co.,
3404 S. Auburn
Kennewick, Washington 99337, USA
tel: (509)-582-3953
Illustrations, including cover, by Don Chandler
of Bellevue, WA
Copyright by Columbia River Book Co.,

Printed in Canada
First edition 2001
Library of Congress Catalog Card Number 2001 130839
ISBN 0-9623556-3-1

All rights including reproduction by
photographic or electronic processes and
translation into other languages are fully
reserved under the International Copyright
Union and International Copyright Convention.

This book is sold subject to the condition
that it shall not be re-sold or otherwise
circulated in any other form without the
publisher's prior consent.

for *Huskies* everywhere.

A real Husky understands it is not the winning or losing that matters in life, but how the game itself is played. *Inest sua gratia parvis*.

Special Acknowledgements
Many people made this book possible by giving the author their time to recall their memories of events in this book. I refer to Husky coaches and players. But a special thanks is given to **Carolyn Marr** of the Seattle Museum of History and Industry and **Jim Daves** of the University of Washington Media Relations Office, who helped locate photographs from their archives for this publication. I am endebted to **Harvey Gover**, Richland, WA for volunteering his editorial services.

Other works by Roger Burke

Novels
The Last Cowboy (1972)
The Out Post Cafe (1974)
A Nice Place To Die (1975)
Beyond Their Country (1976)
The Last Train To Bregenz (1982)
A Home In Bohemia (1991)
The Last Good City (1992)

Collected Stories
Such Young Men (1976)
And Other Americans (1980)

Collected Essays
From The Front (1980)
After Boise There's Pocatello (1988)

Books
Jack Hurley: the last boxing manager alive (1972)
Once A Husky, Always A Husky (2001)

Losing after great striving is the story of man, who was born to sorrow, whose sweetest song tell of saddest thought, and who, if he is a hero, does nothing in life as becoming as leaving it...It is fiercely difficult for the athlete to grow old, but to age with dignity and with courage cuts close to what it is to be a man.

Roger Kahn, - *The Boys Of Summer*

Contents

Introduction

This book is above all an attempt to tell a story. A story of men, most of them young, but some not so young. All of them had a hand in building a tradition, some to a large degree, so their names became familiar to those who read newspapers, and some whose labors and sweat did not get registered even in the footnotes. These men built a tradition in the world of sports.

There are those who think sports are given too much importance in American life, and maybe they're right. Today sports in America is a big business, a multi-billion dollar industry. But in fact, since the time of the ancient Greeks, sports have influenced every society. I have for years considered Edith Hamilton's *The Greek Way* to be one of the most important books I've ever read. In it she reminds us of the value of the games men play:

> *They were the first Westerners; the modern spirit is a Greek discovery...The Greeks were the first people in the world to play, and they played on a grand scale. All over Greece were games, all sorts of games, athletic contests of every description...games so many one grows weary with the list of them...Play died when Greece died and many and many a century passed before it was resurrected.*

If I understand Edith Hamilton correctly, no society or culture can escape the influence of sports - and we can't either, even if we wanted to. Various writers of international reputation and stature have attempted to shed some light on how games and sport influence us. I refer to such writers as Ernest Hemingway and

Albert Camus, both of whom collected Nobel prizes for their work in fiction, but were active in such low brow activities as boxing and bull fighting.

Historically, man seems to be a competitive animal and has been since our earliest origins, and we are no doubt going to continue to be so for as long as we inhabit this globe.

* * * *

Football is a game built upon passion. To tell a story about men involved in it should reveal something of the passions which extend to men at large. It reminds me of what Roger Kahn wrote in his book, *The Boys Of Summer,* about another team many loved, the Brooklyn Dodgers:

> *Losing after striving is the story of man, who was born to sorrow, whose sweetest songs tell of saddest thought, and who, if he is a hero, does nothing in life as becomingly as leaving it.*

So this book was never intended to be a story of all glory and triumphs, but of some bitter losses and defeats, nor a story of all heroes, but of some less than heroic. It tries to tell a story of young men who grew into men after playing a great sport at a large and great university. It attempts to tell a story of how men coached and played a game, and how they lived life after the game. I take my instructions from the wisdom of Edith Hamilton and writers such as Hemingway and Camus who understood how much we can learn from the study of games and the men who play them. If I've read them correctly they were not sure where sports and games end and real life begins. And I've never been sure either.

Roger Burke

The hardest thing to learn in life is which bridge to cross and which to burn.
                    - David Russell

Jim Owens, changed Husky football forever.

Chapter 1
Big Jim In Seattle

In the first place he wasn't from Texas, as the newspapers said, James Donald Owens was born and raised in Oklahoma City, Oklahoma. Nobody knew what his father looked like but the man they called the "Tall Texan" was certainly handsome. At first glance he reminded one of a cross between Cary Grant and John Wayne: his close cropped dark hair crowned a chiseled face that looked a bit too handsome for his profession. He could have been lifted from the cover of one of those paperback Western novels where the hero always has wide shoulders, slim hips, and a jaw that gives a man the expression of both the strength and pathos of a hero. Maybe he should have been in Hollywood.

He came to Seattle to coach a football team. Some local newspapers wrote he was from Texas and thirty years old, but he was neither; he was from Oklahoma and he was two months shy of being thirty. Jim Owens said he was thirty because he figured if people knew he was only twenty-nine some would say he was too young for the job. He wanted the job because it was his first chance to be a head coach after being an assistant for six years under a man they called The Bear. The Bear was Paul (Bear) Bryant who wasn't Hollywood handsome, but he was already starting to accumulate the trappings of a legend as a coach and personality. And Jim Owens who had played college football under another legend, Oklahoma's Bud Wilkinson, had picked up some wisdom from the Bear about how to mold young men into football players and was eager to test what he had learned.

But almost any expert would have told the 'tall Texan' that he had landed in the wrong spot to test himself. He had accepted a job to coach the University of Washington Huskies. There was nothing wrong with the university. The university, established in 1861, nestled in the Northeast side of Seattle on top of a hill that on a clear day revealed a splendid view of Lake Washington and Mt. Rainier beyond the lake. The campus is lush and green and beautiful with enough Gothic styled buildings to make you think you were in Oxford, not Seattle. Seattle was as lush and green and beautiful as any big city in the world. It should have been one of the best coaching jobs in the United States. But it wasn't. In 1957 it was thought of as a dead end job because the Huskies were one of college football's mediocrities and had been for a long time.

That was odd, too, because there was a beautiful horseshoe stadium with a cantilever upper deck that seated 55,000 spectators comfortably. There were enough high schools in the state that if a coach was a decent recruiter and skimmed off most of the blue chippers and then reached down into California and brought back what he couldn't get at home, he should have had a team to compete with any college in the country. But the University of Washington had not been to the Rose Bowl since 1936, the year Jim Owens was nine years old. They found ways to be mediocre, just like the St. Louis Browns or Chicago Cubs. It seemed to be their fate.

Truthfully no one ever thought Washington would have a football program at the same level with the glamour teams of the West Coast, UCLA and Southern Cal, let alone some of the national powers in the middle west and East. In fact, while UCLA, Southern Cal, and even Cal at Berkeley, were glamorous schools, in football they were clearly a cut beneath those from America's heartland. In 1946 the West Coast schools, then called the Pacific Coast Conference, signed an agreement with the Big Ten Conference to match their champions annually in the Rose Bowl and it became a one sided competition with the boys from the heartland winning every year except in 1953. So the smart guys who were in the know about such thing stifled a yawn when an unknown 'Tall Texan' was announced as the fifth coach in 10 years at Washington. With a knowing smile they could have told Jim Owens that his former teammate at Oklahoma, Darrell Royal, had stayed just one year as coach before he hightailed it out in 1956 to take a job at Texas. Maybe this new Texan might last two years, they might have added with a smirk, before he left.

* * * *

It was Owens' misfortune, they might have said, that he wasn't offered the job at University of Houston, which was considering

Owens for the vacant spot there. Instead Houston hired someone named Harold Lahar. Too bad, they would have snickered because Washington still had another year of probation to serve after being caught in 1956 for allowing twenty-seven football players to receive illegal money from boosters. It was called the "Slush Fund," operated by some Seattle downtown boosters. Part of the punishment was that no Washington team could be considered for any championship for two years. The smart guys would add, "That's no punishment: when's the last time Washington won a championship in anything?" Some punishment.

They would have been shocked if they had heard the thoughts of Jim Owens. Owens actually wanted the Washington job more than the job at Houston. He saw Seattle wasn't St. Louis. He saw the big beautiful stadium and the campus. And at Texas A&M, where he had been an assistant under Bear Bryant, he remembered how they had won the Southwestern Conference championship with only twenty-nine players who survived Bryant's boot camp style training regiment. If it could work at Texas A&M, Owens believed, it could work at Washington.

George Briggs Jr., only thirty-two, had offered the job to Owens. Until 1956 he had been the Assistant Athletic Director at the University of California in Berkeley and when the job opened up at Washington, after the football scandal and probation, he accepted their offer. Again a lot of people in the know would have snickered: why leave a soft spot at Berkeley to preside over a sick program at Washington? Briggs didn't see it that way: he was, like Owens, young and looking for a place to be his own man and to test his wings. His first hire was Darrell Royal, who left Mississippi State to come to Seattle. Royal who was a real Texan, jilted the Huskies when the Texas job opened nine months later. Royal had mentioned Owens, his former teammate at Oklahoma, among others, to Briggs before he left. So the merry-go-round continued in Seattle.

Briggs offered the job to Owens at $15,000 a year based on a three year contract. In February Jim Owens, his wife Martha, and their two daughters, Leslie and Kathy, boarded a plane in Dallas, flew to Los Angeles, where they changed planes, and arrived after dark in a snow storm in Seattle. It was a slight improvement over when Owens arrived for his first look at Seattle and the university in January and met Briggs: that day the airline had lost his suitcase and he had no change of clothing for his interview.

Owens had met his wife when they were students at Classen High School in Oklahoma City, where he was a star football player on the team which won the state championship his senior year. After graduating in 1944, Owens went into the Navy Air Corp for two years. They were married in 1947; he was nineteen and she was eighteen. Owens then enrolled at Oklahoma and played for Bud Wilkinson where Owens was named to several All-American teams. Owens thought about studying law, and during his senior year at Oklahoma he took some pre-law courses, but when he had a chance to play some professional football he took it and they moved to Baltimore. It was in Baltimore that Owens got his first taste of coaching when he coached at John Hopkins part time and continued to flirt with the idea of studying law. Then in 1951 he got a call from Paul (Bear) Bryant to join him at Kentucky as an assistant. Owens accepted and he and Martha packed up to move to Lexington. They were pleasant years at Lexington for the Owens family, but in 1954 Texas A&M offered Bryant a job and he accepted it as a move up the coaching ladder. Bryant, a native of Arkansas, probably felt he was getting closer to his roots. Bryant asked Owens to come with him and Owens and family once again packed their bags and headed for College Station, Texas. College Station is located somewhat in the center of a triangle that stretches between Houston at one corner, San Antonio at the other, and Dallas at the top. Not as green as Lexington, it is not as barren as West Texas. It is a college town. Owens watched as once again Bear Bryant began building a program by first weeding out those he considered unable to make a full commitment to his style of football: bare knuckled and take no prisoners. Many did decide to take their careers elsewhere. But by 1956 the resurrection was complete when the Aggies won the conference championship with only twenty-nine players! It impressed Owens.

At about the same time George Briggs Jr. called Jim Owens in College Station, Harry Fouke the Athletic Director at Houston also called. Fouke was also talking to another Oklahoma graduate, Harold Lahar, who was the football coach at Colgate. Fouke chose Lahar and Briggs chose Jim Owens. One bridge burned, one crossed.

Harold Lahar made no lasting changes at Houston, in fact, after the 1961 season he returned to coaching at quiet Colgate. But as Jim and Martha Owens were settling into their house in Northeast Seattle with their two girls, just minutes away from the campus and the big stadium with the upper deck which can be seen for miles like the jutting jaw of some prehistoric reptile, big changes were about to begin at the University of Washington which would forever change its image with both alumni and admirers and its opponents who would come to envy and despise it.

Character is destiny.
- Heraclitus

Jim Owens' first meeting with Huskies

Chapter 2
Some Good Ol' Boys

During the first wet winter weeks in Seattle as Jim and Martha
Owens settled into their house, Owens began putting together his
coaching staff. He naturally turned toward those he knew best.
The first selection was Tom Tipps, 38, who had gone to Sul Ross,

7

and had been at Texas A&M with Owens under Bryant. Bert Clark, 28, Oklahoma '52; Dick Heatly, 28, Oklahoma '52; Harold (Chesty) Walker, 50, Hardin Simmons '31. And the one Washington native, Norm Pollom, 32, a successful high school coach from Aberdeen.

It was an interesting mixture of men and personalities. Owens knew, of course, his first job would be to change the attitude of his players. As in all other endeavors of life, some would change and some wouldn't. Tipps, with perpetual shadows under his eyes, was the designated drill sergeant and defensive specialist. Crewcut Bert Clark had an infectious grin, but could cut either way from a drill sergeant to a guy who could sling an arm around a players shoulders like a good ol' boy and give him a pep talk. Chesty Walker was not merely the oldest coach on the staff, but with his white hair, spectacles, twinkle in his eye, and a Texas drawl that was as thick as gravy, looked like the favorite uncle every boy wanted. But looks were deceiving; Walker was one of the most successful high school football coaches in all of Texas, who came from the panhandle town of Phillips. Heatly was the clean cut All-American boy who players found easy to approach, and was low key. Owens was not an aloof field general in a tower but employed a hands on approach where he often demonstrated the techniques he had learned at Oklahoma and Texas A&M and demanded his players learn too.

After spring practice Owens was mildly surprised to find some good players scattered throughout the squad but two weaknesses were glaring: lack of depth and attitude. He would correct their attitude during the fall camp. The critical moment came just one week before the season opener against the Colorado Buffaloes. After a Saturday scrimmage between the purples, the first team, and the golds, the second team, some players later said the coaches were unhappy with the scrimmage and led the team out of the stadium to a practice field. There the coaches, lead by Owens, began running them up and down the field in fifteen yards sprints.

They ran and ran and ran until players began dropping out. It wasn't that the Huskies were poorly conditioned, in fall camp all had already lost considerable weight and were leaned to a fine point. Typical was guard Don Armstrong who had played at 195 and was down to 177. Duane Lowell, an end, who had played the year before at 200, was barely above 180. As one player explained, they started in a three point stance and when Owens blew his whistle they had to spring fifteen yards and resume a three point. They would run the length of the field and then run back, up and back, up and back. Owens was a participant by running backwards with the players. No one remembers how long it lasted, but the next day *Seattle Post-Intelligencer* sports writer Mike Donohoe termed what he had witnessed as a "death march," because of the fact so many of the players literally dropped out by exhaustion flat on their faces. And forever after it was known as the infamous *Death March*. Some were bitter about it and some accepted it. Luther Carr, a black halfback from Tacoma and the fastest man on the squad said years later to *Seattle Times* sports writer Dick Rockne, "Owens destroyed the team that day. He broke the spirit of the players and he lost their cooperation. A lot of them felt he had been unfair."

Owens tried to explain to the press by what he had seen work at Texas A&M: "You take guys to the point where they think they can't go any further. You can't find out about them until they actually know they can't do it, mentally and physically.... That's when you find out what guys really want to play ball. You always have a few who drop out."

Others weren't so sanguine and dropped out altogether from the Washington program by turning in their gear and transferring to another school. Some like end Duane Lowell, who had to be taken to Providence Hospital and given intravenous fluids after the *Death March*, returned and survived to endure miles more of wind sprints and other soul testing regiments. It is unknown what effect it had on the highly recruited crop of freshmen that Owens and his staff had brought to Washington. They were said to be the most talented group recruited in many years. They had not practiced with the varsity players and missed the *Death March*, but surely they had to have heard about its results and the stories which circulated down to their chambers in the dressing area.

Tom Tipps, not unexpectedly, having seen the results at Texas A&M recalled something similar in his days as a player at Sul Ross, a small college tucked away in insular Alpine, Texas. He told a Seattle newspaper, "One day our coach heard about some players who had broken training and he figured if he punished everyone he'd learn who the guilty were. He started running us at four in the afternoon with a 440 yard, then sprints of twenty yards, punctuated by falling flat on your stomach. At the end of a football field of sprints he had us run another 440. In the first ten minutes three players passed out. Three hours later we were still running. But not another man passed out. There was a great difference in our strength and endurance, but it was stubbornness that kept each of us going. Some call that mental toughness. I hated the coach for it, but he taught me a great thing that day. I learned the body is a lot tougher than the mind knows. I never forgot that lesson."

Whatever, it didn't seem to help against the Colorado Buffaloes. On a bright Saturday afternoon perfect for college football, 34,000 fans were curious enough to witness a 6-6 tie. From the fifty-three players who showed up for the first day of fall practice there were thirty-seven who suited up for Colorado. The Jim Owens era had begun at Washington. The next week in Minneapolis the Huskies were beaten 46-7 by Minnesota. Minnesota was quarterbacked by a former Husky, Bobby Cox, who transferred before Owens arrived. The next week in Seattle another group of Big Ten boys, Ohio State, tattooed the Huskies 35-7. UCLA followed them into town and being one of the conference favorites it looked like another behind the barn fanny whipping, but the final score was somewhat respectable 19-0. After four weeks the new era totaled

20 points for the Huskies and 106 for opponents. The *Death March* and extra conditioning didn't seem to be paying any dividends. Enter Stanford lead by All-American quarterback John Brodie. The Huskies lost by a respectable 21-14 margin.

Next up was defending Pacific Coast Champion Oregon State. The Beavers were solid favorites over the winless Huskies in Seattle, but in a major upset Washington beat the Beavers 19-7. The next week Southern Cal came to town, but the Huskies couldn't summon another upset and lost 19-12. Washington visited Portland the following Saturday for a game with Oregon, who would eventually win the conference crown and represent the league in the Rose Bowl against Ohio State. Once again the Huskies found a way to an upset over a highly favored team 13-6. The Oregon win was capped with a 35-27 win over California in Berkeley. The season ended in a 27-7 thrashing by arch rival Washington State in front of their largest home crowd of the season, 47,352.

During the winter that followed it could have been surmised that Jim Owens and his staff were discouraged by the fact they had won but three games and tied one. But that was not the case, not in the mind of Owens who believed they had taken the first step by building in their players a kind of character that is necessary to winning. For some this price was not only too high but too painful and they voted with their feet to desert Seattle. But for the man from Oklahoma there was no despair or doubts for he truly believed *character was destiny*. As a disciple of the Bear it was not blind faith but a living ethos that he had witnessed work wonders in College Station. He was going to make believers in Seattle sooner than anyone imagined. Perhaps even sooner than he imagined.

One man with courage makes a majority.
- Andrew Jackson

Chapter 3
September, 1958

They were green as grass, Owens knew. They had no experience at quarterback. He could start the more experienced players who had been through the 1957 season with him or go with the sophomores, who were more talented but without a single down of varsity playing experience. Owens went with his gut feeling and started 10 sophomores and one senior, Don Armstrong, to start the opening game against San Jose State in Husky Stadium. A sleepy crowd of 29,395 showed up to watch a sleepy game which Washington won 14-6. The next game was at home against Minnesota, the Golden Gophers had walloped the Huskies the year before in Minneapolis 46-7. Before 38,716, Washington stunned the Gophers 24-21. Owens felt some vindication for having gone with the youth program, but another test loomed ahead: Rose Bowl champion Ohio State like a Minotaur waited for Washington in Columbus. Like Minnesota, Ohio State had blown out the Huskies in 1957, 35-7, and there was no reason to believe it would be any different in Columbus.

It is hard to say what makes a group of men come together as a team with a personality. But already this green group of fuzzy cheeked young men were forming a personality which the Minnesota game revealed glimpses of. There were no great athletes in the group. They were not even large by college standards of 1958, if anything they were on the small side as far as weight goes. But they were going to make opponents earn every yard by paying for it with black and blue marks. They had as a group accepted the Owens' philosophy which was borrowed from Bear Bryant at Texas A&M: take no prisoners.

The Ohio State stadium in Columbus seats 85,000 and if there was a place where a young team that started ten sophomores was going to get stage freight and come apart, it was in Columbus. Instead, before 79,477, the Huskies played like veterans and carried the fight to the highly favored Buckeyes on every down. At the end Ohio State escaped the misfortune of Minnesota, but only by a 12-7 score. And there were plenty of bruised ribs to nurse following their escape. Clearly things had changed. Now it was time to settle some scores back in the conference.

But what the Huskies excelled at in grit and gameness they still lacked in polished skills and experience, and in their first conference game at Stanford the Indians prevailed 22-12. Next was UCLA, who had recorded the only shut out against them the previous year. And once again UCLA was able to blank the Huskies, this time 20-0. Next up was Oregon State in Portland and this time the Beavers extracted revenge for being upset the previous year. The final was 14-12. The highlight of the season turned out to be the next game, a win over Oregon. Sophomore quarterback Bob Hivner completed a short screen pass to Luther Carr who out sprinted the entire Oregon defense to score the game's only touchdown, giving the Huskies a 6-0 win over the defending conference champions. California who would replace Oregon as conference champion. Like Ohio State, California would escape with a 12-7 victory but leave with some sore ribs and a respect for the young gang of Jim Owens.

The season finale was in Spokane against the Washington State Cougars. Just as Minnesota and Ohio State had an easy time against the Huskies the year before, so had the Cougars, and their 1958 team was a veteran team led by quarterback Bobby Newman and end Gail Cogdill, a future All-Pro for the Detroit Lions. The Cougars escaped with a narrow win 18-14 and some bruised ribs.

The conference should have taken notice that with the exception of the UCLA game a group of green sophomores had roughed up and made every team sweat out narrow wins. What they lacked was obvious: the know how to score points, which comes only with game experience. The Huskies scored only 102 points for the season, the lowest total since the 1954 squad scored but 78 in the disastrous season under John Cherberg.

But one Seattle sports writer, Emmett Watson of the *Seattle Post-Intelligencer*, caught a glimpse of the future ahead of the other local writers. Forty years later when the 1959 team had a reunion Watson wrote about what he'd witnessed:

> "The Dogs lost games of course (1957 and 1958). But something was clearly going on; something we hadn't seen before. The Huskies' losing side was usually tight-lipped and angry, as though losing was the most unthinkable, repulsive thing that could happen.
>
> "Once I asked a Husky player what the high point of that day's game was. He said, 'When that blank-blank guy' - he named a star running back for the other team - 'took himself out of the game. We punished him, we forced him to quit.'
>
> "I also had to cover the winners' dressing room. It was like taking a notepad into the Harborview emergency ward on a busy night.
>
> "Players - winning players - were beat up, bruised, exhausted, sometimes stunned by what they had been through. Instead of exulting, they were moaning. That's what the Huskies were doing to teams they lost to."

For Owens, as the winter clouds banked in from the Pacific and colored the days a uniform gloomy gray over Seattle, he was not seeing gloom or gray. Jim Owens green troops had stood up to the baptism of fire and he felt the next year when his troops took the field the paybacks would begin.   In fact, it is fair to say no one expected what would happen the next season. Not Emmett Watson, or any of the other Seattle sports writers, or the sharps downtown who covered bets on the ponies and world series and football games.

Sometimes *one man with courage* does make a majority.   But when you have eleven men with raw courage ready to lay it on the line on every play you have a demolition team in cleats and a football game can look more like a demolition derby.

When Jim Owens and his staff first arrived in 1957 their offices were in small drafty cubicles in a barn-like building called Hec Edmundson Pavilion, where varsity basketball games had been played since 1923. Then they were moved down to a wooden shed on the practice field that had once been a World War II prisoner of war camp! In that wooden shed, like a Robespierre, men were plotting a revolution to overthrow royalty. For a revolution to succeed it always takes *one man with courage to make a majority.* Jim Owens was the one man.

A hero is no braver than an ordinary man, but he is braver five minutes longer. "
- Ralph Waldo Emerson

Chapter 4
Such Young Men

No one has ever been able to explain or illuminate to the satisfaction of skeptics why some teams taken as a whole are so much greater than their individual parts. For lack of a better explanation scribes have used the word chemistry. Some teams, they say, have better chemistry. So they excel. David Halberstram in his book *Summer of '49* explained that the Boston Red Sox were, to a man, position by position, superior to any other American League team in 1949, including the New York Yankees. And everyone has agreed, but it was the Yankees who ended up in the world series and not Boston.

In football, a group of men literally sweat and bleed together, often eat and sleep together, and get to know each other to a degree that is only common in one other fraternity: military life. Ask any combat soldier and he will tell you if your life depends on the man next to you in a foxhole, you'd better know and trust him better than your girlfriend or wife.

Football, like war, is a series of skirmishes by squad sized units. And just as in the military, every squad needs a leader. In football, the squad or platoon leader is usually the quarterback, because he calls the plays in the huddle. As the Washington Huskies entered the 1959 season, Owens and his staff already knew from the previous year when they started 10 sophomores that their defense was rock solid. No team was going to be able to score many points against them, but it was the offense that was

16

the concern.

They had two quarterbacks who were nearly identical in talent and skills; **Bob Hivner**, from Los Angeles, and **Bob Schloredt**, from Gresham, Oregon a suburb of Portland. Hivner had started most of the games the year before. He was slightly smaller and slightly more nimble than Schloredt. Bob Hivner grew up dreaming about becoming a Washington Husky because as a boy he had admired Don Heinrich, the All-American Washington quarterback of the early '50s. So for Hivner his dream was coming true: Owens named Hivner to start the opening game at Colorado. Washington entered the game as a slight underdog both because of the fact Colorado was one of the better teams in the Big-Eight Conference and because the game was at Boulder. Washington won 21-12, but an injury happened that was to change the rest of the season and perhaps the future of Washington football. Bob Hivner broke his thumb and Schloredt moved up to the starter.

On the battlefield when a squad or platoon leader is a casualty he is replaced from within the ranks, but it's never known if the men will have the same confidence in him. So it was with Schloredt. Under Schloredt's leadership, the offense began coming together in ways that only the naked eye could detect because the results were too subtle to show up in raw statistics. If the Huskies needed three yards for a first down Schloredt found a way to get four or five yards. If they needed a first down to keep a critical drive going, he would get it. Adding to the mystery was the fact that the offense under Owens required the quarterback to do a good deal of running on option plays, and Schloredt didn't have sprinter's speed. But at slightly over six feet tall and weighing 195 pounds Schloredt had deceptive strength so that he seldom went down on first contact and was able time after time to take a hit and pick up additional yardage. This tends to take the starch out of a defense. As a passer Schloredt was average, but maybe shouldn't have been even that because a childhood accident with a firecracker had damaged most of the vision out of one eye. So he was called, of course, the one-eyed quarterback. He had declared pre-dentistry as his major of study.

The backfield was another oddity because it included several junior college transfers new to the system and the oldest man on the team, **Don McKeta**, twenty-four, from McKeesports, Pennsylvania, who had spent several years in the Navy. McKeta had gotten out of the Navy in California after playing several years of Navy football and drawing attention of several NFL talent scouts. But after sitting in the Rose Bowl in 1958 and watching Oregon play Ohio State, McKeta had his heart set on being an Oregon Duck - but Coach Len Casanova at Oregon never recruited McKeta and at the ripe old age of twenty-three McKeta drove north to Seattle to enroll at Washington as a sophomore in August, 1958. He quickly fit into the system where only the most durable could survive. McKeta declared Business Administration as his major study.

Ray Jackson, from Waco, Texas, was one of only a handful of black players, and another junior college transfer. He was listed as a fullback, but once again didn't fit the mold of what a fullback was supposed to be: he was stumpy at five feet nine inches and at 180 pounds, light for the position. Jackson did not declare a major study.

George Flemming, from Los Angeles, was another junior college transfer, a halfback with a deceptive flowing style of running that made him look slower than he was. He looked willowy at six foot and 180 pounds and excelled at making tacklers miss, especially in the open field, returning punts and kickoffs. Flemming declared no major study.

Lee Folkins, end, from Seattle's Roosevelt High School, was the first Husky recruited by Owens' staff in 1957. Folkins was built more like a basketball player at six feet five inches and 200 pounds. He was probably the best pass receiver on the starting team. Folkins declared Electrical Engineering as his major.

Kurt Gegner, tackle, was also from Seattle's Roosevelt High School where he had played with Folkins, but his background was unusual. His parents had perished in Germany during World War II and he ended up an orphan in America. For his position, Gegner was also slightly undersized at six feet two inches and 205 pounds. But there was no more aggressive and determined player on the team than Gegner. He declared Mechanical Engineering as his major.

Chuck Allen, guard, came from a small town nestled in the Cascade mountains called Cle Elum, once a coal mining center. He was a fine all-around athlete, quick on his feet, and average size for his position, at six feet one inch and 205 pounds. Allen had declared Business Administration as his major.

Roy McKasson, center, was from Tacoma and was like other Huskies somewhat undersized for his position at six feet one inch and 195 pounds, but he was extremely aggressive. He was also vocal in the huddle when it seemed the team needed some encouragement. McKasson was a Business Administration student.

Bill Kinnune, guard, from Everett, a city north of Seattle, was good sized for his position at six feet two inches and 220 pounds. He was quiet and steady and one of the better blockers on the line. He was also a Business Administration student.

Barry Bullard, tackle, from Coos Bay, Oregon, was good sized for his position at six feet four and 225 pounds. An excellent blocker, Bullard declared Engineering as his major.

John Meyers, end, from Richland, was the largest player on the starting team at six feet six inches and two hundred and twenty-five pounds. He was said to be the strongest player. Meyers was also a good all-around athlete having played basketball in high school for three years and in his senior year played center on his team which won the Washington State high school championship. In fact, Meyers did not play freshman football at Washington and instead concentrated on basketball, but turned out for football during the spring and won a starting spot. He was the lone sophomore on the first team, all the others being juniors. Meyers declared construction management as his major.

It is said football is a game of trench warfare and that games are most often won or lost in the trenches. So it would seem to understand the success of this team one would have to start by studying the men up front in the trenches. As a group they were tall and rangy, but not heavy. They were almost to a man all-around athletes and not to be overlooked they were as a group very bright and quick learners. Because of that they were not prone to make mistakes at critical times. Had they played at another school away from the demanding practices under Owens they would have probably weighed and played ten or fifteen pounds heavier. But Owens had run them lean and mean. One player, John Meyers, years later told Dick Rockne of the *Seattle Times*: "In our practices we had fights, lots of fights. Not just one player against another but unit against unit. The coaches used to get right in and fight too. And afterwards we'd all laugh about it."

At first glance that method of building character would seem zany if not the way to produce thugs instead of college athletes, but somehow it brought the team closer together rather than driving them apart.

The key reserves. **Jim Skaggs**, guard, six feet one inches and 210 pounds from Arroyo Grande, California was a sophomore who seemed to thrive under the Marine boot camp atmosphere. Skaggs could relieve either Kinnune or Allen without a drop off in intensity or efficiency.

Joe Jones, fullback, from Los Angeles was a junior college transfer, who could relieve Ray Jackson. Jones was more traditional for a fullback in running style and size.

Stan Chapple, end, from Seattle, was almost an identical twin to Lee Folkins at six feet four inches and 210 pounds.

George Pitt, center, was a six foot, 200 pound senior from Yakima. A ferocious hitter, Pitt and McKasson waged the most intense duels in the Owens' challenge system where any player could challenge the purple jersey holder for his starting position. In the challenge system each player had to go one on one and had three charges on offense and three on defense. Pitt was an excellent baseball player and had come to Washington to play baseball. Like so many Huskies linemen Pitt was a converted fullback.

Dave Enslow, guard-tackle, was a six foot, 210 pound lineman who also participated in wrestling. He was a junior from Seattle.

Ben Davidson, end, six feet seven inches, 235 pounds, a junior college transfer from Southern California, was a work in progress. He hadn't played football in high school and had played only one year at a junior college. He would later achieve more recognition as a professional at Oakland than he ever did in college as a reserve. In spots he filled in well for his twin, John Meyers.

These were the key players as the 1959 season began. There was no great player among them, but there was a high level of all-around athletes, a high level of intelligence in places where you would not expect to find it in football, in the trenches. The oldest player, a Navy veteran, was in the backfield and the quarterback planned to become a dentist. There didn't seem to be a hero among them nor any All-Americans, but as a group they had a personality that demanded they were going to be braver than anyone else for *five minutes longer*. Later sports writers would call them the team named desire, but in fact they were young men who determined their own destiny by being guttier than whoever lined up across the trenches from them.

As life is action and passion, it is required of man that he should share the passion and action of his time. "
- Oliver Wendell Holmes

Chapter 5
September, 1959

In America the autumn of 1959 was ushered in with a baseball race that would end up with the Los Angeles Dodgers playing the Chicago White Sox in the world series. With the presidential race still a year away Senator John F. Kennedy was maneuvering around Senator Hubert Humphrey to position himself for a 1960 presidential run. President Eisenhower was concentrating on his golf game while Vice-President Richard Nixon was putting together his election staff. It was not a period of passion or action in the United States. The sputnik excitement of 1957 was over and the U.S. was concentrating on developing Jupiter rockets for their own satellites. In Hollywood, *Ben Hur*, staring Charlton Heston, would win an Oscar for Best Picture. One of the best selling books of 1959 was an old tome, *Lady Chatterley's Lover*; it was banned until 1959 in the U.S., although it had originally been published in England in 1923. One of the most popular songs of the year was the Kingston Trio's *Hang Down Your Head Tom Dooley*, a folk song that dated back to the mid-1800's. In boxing, Floyd Patterson was rendered ex-heavyweight champion by a Swede named Johansson. Cassius Clay was still a teenager boxing amateurs in Louisville, Kentucky, and Sonny Liston was trying to stay out of jail in St. Louis. In Kansas City a little known twenty-four year-old outfielder named Roger Maris was playing baseball for the Kansas City Athletics. In West Germany a tank driver named Elvis Presley was making $105 a month in the Army. In Detroit Robert McNamera was still at Ford and making Edsels.

22

Few people in America knew or cared who Martin Luther King was. On September 11 at El Toro Marine Station in California, an obscure Marine named Lee Harvey Oswald was discharged routinely and then defected to Russia. Vietnam was a place on the map called Indo-China. It was a time when America was caught between the old and the new. There was a feeling of a tide going out, but no one was sure what the new tide coming in was carrying. It was not exaggeration to say that America in 1959 was a slumbering giant. Just ahead were unthinkable changes in politics, sports, and culture to awaken the giant with a bang.

* * * *

In Seattle, Jim Owens and his staff were getting ready to start the football season full of quiet confidence. It had been a pleasant summer for Owens and his family. Chesty Walker was still driving his purple and white Thunderbird and still trying to quit smoking. As he told Bert Clark in his dry Texas humor one September afternoon, "I've got such a back ache that I went to the doctor and you know what he told me, Bert? He said I shouldn't pick up anything heavier than a cigarette, a king sized cigarette." Tom Tipps was still plotting new defenses. Bert Clark was discovering the joys of golf. Seattle was enjoying a robust economy with Boeing producing their 707 jet liners. The enrollment at the University of Washington was 22,000 undergraduates and tuition cost a student $150 for one quarter! Seattle seemed to mirror the United States as a whole: all quiet on the Western front.

Several days before the Colorado game Owens explained his optimism about the coming season to a *Seattle Times* reporter this way, "I don't know what they've got, but I know what we've got."

Awareness and perseverance are not enough to help one resist and survive if the times in which one lives are contrary to those that are ahead. A man can fight everything except his own times.

Milovan Djilas, - *Land Without Justice*

Chapter 6
Jim Owens 1959-1974

There have been few college football teams who experienced a football season such as the Washington Huskies experienced in 1959. It is, of course, uplifting in all sports at all levels when the perennial loser suddenly becomes a champion. Nothing is so dear in American life as the underdog. So the Huskies of 1959 not only won the hearts of those in Seattle but those in distant points from Seattle. It wasn't just that they won every game except one on their schedule, it was how they won their games that impressed. Four teams were shut out and four other teams could score but a single touchdown against the Huskies.

Every game was a kind of game where the Huskies seemed more intent on putting players in the first aid ward than winning the game. It was clean but brutal football. After the demolition of Wisconsin in the Rose Bowl, 44-8, it also lifted Jim Owens from obscurity to national attention. Suddenly the name Jim Owens was not only known in Seattle, but across the American sports landscape. Just as suddenly the Huskies went from being the Chicago Cubs of football to the winner's circle. They were clear favorites to repeat as Pacific champions and play in the Rose Bowl once again as they returned for the 1960 season, every starter not only on the first team purple unit, but every member of the second unit gold team. In a word this was a deep team, the down side was

24

that every team on their schedule now saw the Huskies as the one team they wanted to beat.

The schedule was favorable as the non-conference games were College of Pacific, Idaho, and Navy - all at home - before opening the conference at Stanford. Only Navy seemed likely to give the Huskies a work out they needed before the conference opener. There were some scribes who suggested that the team which surrendered only 73 points the whole of the 1959 season might actually go unscored on during 1960. It was unrealistic of course. Pacific spoiled that by scoring late in the game against Husky reserves. Idaho also scored not once but twice late in the game against Husky reserves. Then it was Navy's turn and 57,379, a new stadium record, turned out to see the Midshipmen from Annapolis play in Seattle for the first time. The Huskies were solid favorites. But despite the fact the Huskies drove up and down the field, they couldn't put any distance between themselves and the pesky Navy team, lead by Heisman candidate running back Joe Bellino. Late in the 4th quarter the Huskies held onto a slim 14-12 lead with Bob Schloredt back to punt. The hike from center was low and bounced twice before Schloredt could scoop it up and was tackled at the Washington 24. Still, with a little over one minute to play it seemed the Huskies could hang on. Navy quarterback Hal Spooner completed a pass in the end zone for what appeared to be the winning score. But a penalty canceled the score and Greg Mather's 4th down kick from the Navy 32 yard line sailed true with 14 seconds showing on the stadium clock. The record crowd was stunned by the sudden turn of events. This was a game that should never have been lost. A quick glance at the final game stats made one wonder how Navy had even scored. Bellino was held to 53 yards rushing for the game and in total offense Washington had a 193-69 margin which usually is good for a comfortable win. But gone was the unbeaten season so many had hoped for.

The Husky dressing room was equally hushed. Navy was far

from the strongest team the Huskies would face in 1960 and yet the Huskies had managed to lose a game they had dominated in every aspect. To a man, there was a sense of disbelief in the Husky dressing room. As the sound of plastic helmets and shoulder pads clattered against the concrete floor naked men avoided each others eyes. After all the blood and sweat they had gone through in the previous two years together the idea of losing had become something unthinkable.

That October 1 game with Navy turned out to be the low point of 1960, but it should have been a warning to every Husky player, coach, and fan: no matter how hard the struggle to reach the top, once there the struggle to remain on top was just as fierce. That's what being champion meant. The Huskies would win three games in 1960 by the margin of a single point and have to come behind to do that against their neighborhood rivals Oregon State, Oregon and Washington State. They would see the injury bug rise up to bite them over and over as linemen John Meyers, Bill Kinnune, Barry Bullard, Kurt Gegner, Jim Skaggs, and Chuck Allen would all miss at least two games with injuries. This was the heart and soul of the Husky team: the men in the trenches. In addition, All-American quarterback Bob Schloredt broke his collarbone in the fifth game against UCLA and was lost for the season. It must have seemed to the coaches that fate had decided to work against them repeating as champions.

But the 1960 Huskies won more on sheer grit than anything else as they turned back challenge after challenge such as the Oregon State game in Portland. Oregon State coached by Tommy Prothro had a new weapon in 1960 with the introduction of a brilliant sophomore tailback named Terry Baker. Baker, who would later win the Heisman Trophy in 1962, was a left handed passer and much more agile than his gangly six foot three frame would appear him to be. A week after losing Schloredt, the Huskies arrived in Portland for their annual tradition visit to ancient Multnomah Stadium. A crowd of 36,833 was crammed into the old baseball park as the Beaver partisans sensed the Huskies were ripe for an upset on the heels of losing their All-American quarterback. And it surely seemed that way as the Huskies had to fight back from 12-0 and then 23-7 deficits and had to score the winning touchdown with less than three minutes in the game on a quarterback sneak by Schloredt's replacement, Bob Hivner. The Oregon State game was in a sense a precursor for the remainder of the season. While the Huskies were healthy and practically injury free in 1959 they were crippled and limping in 1960. But at the end, they were once again 9-1, and champions and Pasadena bound; this time to play what was considered the number one team in the nation, Minnesota. And once again Owens' troops found themselves solid underdogs to the boys from the American heartland. And once again they proved the experts wrong, this time by a 17-7 score.

The next year Owens and his staff found themselves in a rebuilding situation. Graduated was every starter on the purple unit, but one, and the second unit, the gold team too. Both Hivner and Schloredt were also graduated. Not surprisingly they finished 5-4-1, but surprisingly they came within a whisker of returning to the Rose Bowl. A 0-0 tie with Southern Cal in Seattle was the fly in the ointment. 1962 held out promise of a successful season with many veterans returning from 1961. And it was successful as the Huskies under Owens finished 7-1-2, the single loss being to Southern Cal in Los Angeles. Southern Cal finished the year at 11-0 and National Champions. The 1963 season figured to be the most successful season since the 1961 Rose Bowl team, but it started out as if it was going to be a bust as the Huskies lost their three non-conference games and, in the process scored a grand total of 20 points.

But once again a quirky injury at quarterback turned around the team's fortunes just as did the injury to Bob Hivner in the 1959 season that brought about the emergence of Bob Schloredt. The starting quarterback, Bill Siler, was discovered to have hepatitis and Bill Douglas was promoted to starter. The Huskies began to roll then and only a stumble against UCLA in Los Angeles marred a perfect conference record. Douglas was injured in the opening minutes of the Rose Bowl game with a knee injury as he drove the Huskies down the field to what appeared to be a brilliant opening drive to the Illini 15. Douglas was replaced by Siler. Siler's first pass was caught but, fumbled by end Al Libke, and it was a frustrating and losing afternoon for the Huskies in Pasadena.

Unthinkable, to Husky fans was the fact it was to be the last time a Jim Owens coached Husky team would play in Pasadena. A number of factors seemed to arrive at about the same time to change the formula which Owens had used so successfully to build Washington into a national power.

First, the NCAA rules committee decided prior to the 1964 season to allow unlimited substitution, this was an attempt to juice up the college game and allow more scoring. It was an obvious attempt to copy the professional game. This hurt Owens' philosophy of putting emphasis upon physical conditioning of his players and defense. Not surprisingly the 1964 Husky team led the nation in rushing defense, but could score only 139 points for the season, which left them with a 6-4 record. At the same time, the school administration in an attempt to hold down enrollment imposed a higher admission standard for out-of-state students. This hurt the recruitment for specialized players from out of state to fit the new unlimited substitution rule. One year later the administration once again tightened standards for out-of-state students. This left Washington at a clear recruiting disadvantage to its main rivals at UCLA and Southern Cal. Not surprisingly, both California schools began to dominate the conference and the Rose Bowl at that time.

In what might seem another cruel twist of fate after the Rose Bowl game of 1964 the original group of coaches who came north with Owens in 1957 began to leave Seattle. The first was Bert Clark who accepted the job of head coach at arch rival

Washington State and took with him Dick Heatly. The next to leave was Chesty Walker who left in 1965 to retire to Texas. And finally after a disastrous 1969 season in which the Huskies won but one game, the old martinet and drill sergeant Tom Tipps left.

It must have seemed to Jim Owens that the stars had lined up against him. In fact, it was simply time and events turned so quickly that it only seemed the gods had turned against him. How many Americans in 1960 knew much about a place called Vietnam? How many Americans in 1960 could imagine what social changes would be brought about by the civil rights movement in the American South? It must have seemed to almost every American in 1960 that when 1970 arrived America would be the same place it was in 1960 when in fact in the space of one decade everything had changed in America.

One of the most charismatic presidents of the 20th century, John Kennedy, was murdered and deposed, the next president, Lyndon Johnson, was driven from office by an unpopular war in Vietnam, which he blindly pushed until it consumed him, and the next president, Richard Nixon, was a man who everyone agreed after 1962 had no future whatever in American politics. Into that mix was the assassination of the most powerful force for racial change in American history, Martin Luther King Jr., and race riots in major American cities that stunned Americans to silence.

Jim Owens who grew up in Oklahoma City, which isn't part of the deep south where so much civil unrest took place, but which nevertheless is part of the South, no doubt never dreamed in 1964 that any of the '60s changes would affect his world in Seattle. Seattle seemed far removed from the unrest in Birmingham and Mississippi. Seattle was not to be compared with the unrest in a place such as Berkeley. Seattle was pastoral and isolated from the hotbeds of upheaval. But life is not only unfair, but unpredictable.

The changes no doubt caught Jim Owens from the blind side. He had after all lived sort of a charmed life. When he enlisted in the Navy following his graduation from high school in 1944, he was stationed for a time in Norman, Oklahoma, following his basic training in California. Norman is but a stones throw from Oklahoma City. This was at a time when a lot of boys were still dying in combat in the Pacific theater. After Norman Owens was sent to Corpus Cristi, Texas where he was able to hitchhike home on weekends to see his girlfriend. Owens was married at 19. There followed his marriage and four years of college and playing football at the University of Oklahoma. After a brief fling at professional football in Baltimore, there came a call from Bear Bryant in Lexington, and then on to College Station with the Bear. And finally came the head job at Washington, all before he was thirty years old.

So on March 15 of 1968 when *Life* magazine printed a story about black athletes and discrimination at Washington, Jim Owens must have felt stunned. For the fact is Jim Owens never was a bigot or prejudice in any way. That is not to say he might not have been insensitive to black athletes problems at a largely all white and large university. It was not simply that most of Owens' original staff, Walker, Tipps, Clark, Heatly, were from the South, it is far more likely this group of men, like the vast majority of Americans everywhere, were unaware of black problems and the thinking of Black Americans. It is probably the most difficult of all tasks in life to walk in another man's shoes. Black author James Baldwin in his book *Nobody Knows My Name* wrote:

> *"Negroes want to be treated like men:* a perfectly straight-forward statement, containing only seven words. People who have mastered Kant, Hegel, Shakespeare, Marx, Freud, and the Bible find this statement utterly impenetrable."

It is doubtful that Owens and his staff spent much time with Shakespeare or Marx or Freud, let alone James Baldwin. Their business was to win football games. And even if they had, it is not certain it would have helped. Take the case of A.J. Liebling. Liebling was accorded by everyone who mattered to be one of the best journalists of his time and he was a great war correspondent during World War II from the European theater. Yet in 1956

when British author Graham Greene's novel *The Quiet American*
was published, Liebing was so incensed that he wrote in his
review of the book it was nothing but an anti-American diatribe.
In fact, Greene, who had spent considerable time in Asia and
Indo-China, had witnessed the defeat of the French there, and his
novel was a precursor of what would happen to Americans if they
followed the French into Indo-China. Liebling was offended. He
was also blind, and had he lived long enough, he would have had
to conclude what millions of other Americans had to later admit:
they were also wrong about the question of Vietnam. Liebling,
being a scholar had mastered much of Kant, Hegel, Shakespeare,
Marx, and Freud. But he had never set foot in Vietnam and knew
nothing about the Vietnamese mind or thinking. It was therefore
impossible for him to walk in Vietnamese shoes.

There was, no doubt, after the *Life* magazine story considerable
consternation in the mind of Jim Owens. All his life he had been
a decent man, and then some people were saying the opposite. The
problem escalated when some black football players were
suspended and blacks began calling for Owens to resign. Then in
1969 Owens' oldest daughter, Kathy, was pulled out of her car in
Seattle and assaulted. At that point Jim Owens must have thought
the sky was falling in on him in Seattle. In addition, the 1968 team
was able to win but three games. In Owens' mind things couldn't
get any worse. But he was wrong. In 1969 his Huskies won only
one game.

Enter a sophomore quarterback from a small town in Oregon, an
Indian named Sonny Sixkiller. Under Sixkiller's passing attack
the Huskies fortunes turned around and they won six games and
could easily have won nine games and gone to the Rose Bowl.
During the next two seasons, led by Sixkiller's passing, the
Huskies won 16 games, but could not get to Pasadena. In 1973,
a rebuilding year, the Huskies declined and could win but two
games. In 1974 the Huskies rebounded somewhat under an option
attack featuring quarterback Denny Fitzpatrick and won five

games. But in a surprise announcement Owens announced his retirement at the team's annual banquet in December. He prefaced his announcement by framing them around the words of Henry Wadsworth Longfellow:

> "We are the sum of our days, and should look sharp at how they pass. Of our days, they come and go like muffled and veiled figures sent from a distant friendly party;"

Few would have suspected that Jim Owens read poetry and the words he chose to mark the closing of his career at Washington were enigmatic, if not tinged with pathos. Perhaps all the adversity which came from 1964 onward had conditioned Owens toward the pathos in life. It seemed for so long his star had no limits to how far it would rise. During his senior year in high school Owens' team won the state football championship and he was named All State. In high school he also met and fell in love with the girl he would marry. In the military during the greatest war the world ever saw he was not sent to a hot combat zone, but his first duty station was in Norman, only a few miles from where he grew up. Then during his senior year in college he played on an unbeaten team and was named All-American. Then he was to coach under a man who was to be a legend among coaches, Paul (Bear) Bryant. And at his first head coaching job he turned around a team of perennial also rans and losers and made them into champions within three years. There truly seemed no limit to how high his star would rise.

Then it all began to come apart: the change in the rules, the change in the admission standards, the racial upheaval, and Vietnam. None of those things could he control but all influenced how he could coach and who he could coach. Owens' last season was a losing one, 5 wins and 6 loses. In fact, from 1964 through 1974 his record was 55 wins, 57 loses, and 2 ties. A winning percentage of 48%, just slightly better than the Washington record from 1942 to 1956 of 65 wins, 68 loses and 7 ties, a winning percentage of 46%. Nothing he had learned at Oklahoma under Wilkinson or at Texas A & M under Bear Bryant had prepared him for what he was to experience when the changes came to America in the 1960s. The truth is no man is ever prepared for the great changes when they come. It is an uneven contest between man and the world. The words of Milovan Djilas, who spent many years in jail under communism, the very system he fought so hard to bring to power in Yugoslavia, ring out to any and all who can hear them: *Awareness and perseverance are not enough to help one resist and survive if the times in which one lives are contrary to those that are ahead. A man can fight everything except his own times.*

There is always the illusion that we control our times, but it is only an illusion. None of us are ever ready for the great changes when they come, because we cannot see them until like a wave they have rolled over us.

Exile has been written about since Cain and Abel in the Bible, but no one has written with more grace and poetry about the state of the exile than the late Yugoslav writer Milovan Djilas. His classic book, *The Leper And Other Stories*, is out of print and no doubt hard to find even in public libraries, but the reward for finding and reading it is great. Djilas journey in life was first as a student revolutionary, then as a partisan guerilla, then after seeing what he had struggled to bring to power turn corrupt, he found himself a political prisoner behind bars by the same powers he had brought to power.

I have often thought of Jim Owens as a kind of exile, although from his beautiful home at the head of Flathead Lake in western Montana, it might seem a royal exile. And since he resigned as coach in 1974 a case could be made that he is anything but an exile. But a coach is no different than a great military leader: they are considered successful only if they lead their troops to great victories not stalemates. Jim Owens final season at the school where he had built a great tradition was at best a stalemate. And no doubt until the final hour Owens was puzzled by his fate.

For over a thousand years Roman conquerors returning from the wars, enjoyed the honor of triumph, the tumultuous parade. In the procession came trumpeters, musicians and strange animals from the conquered territories. The conqueror rode in the triumphant chariot...A slave behind the conqueror holding a golden crown and whispering in his ear a warning: that all glory is fleeting."
- General George S. Patton

Don James, the most successful Husky football coach ever.

Chapter 7
Don James 1975-1992

The man who was chosen to succeed Jim Owens was his opposite   physically; while Owens was a imposing figure stretching out to six feet four inches, Don James was a good six inches shorter. James grew up in the upper middle West in Massillon, Ohio, (pop. 32, 000) where he played quarterback on two state championship football teams at Washington High School. After high school in Ohio, James accepted a scholarship to Miami, Florida and played quarterback there setting a number of passing records. After graduation he spent the next two years in the US Army as a Lieutenant and then enrolled at the University of Kansas to work on a Master's degree in Education, where he graduated in 1957.

James then returned to south Florida to coach high school football for two years and then jumped into the college ranks, beginning as an assistant at Florida State (1959-65), Michigan (1966-67), and Colorado (1968-70). In 1971 he landed his first head coaching spot at Kent State in Ohio. James stayed at Kent State for four years before he answered the call to Seattle and the Huskies several days before Christmas 1974.

Unlike Owens who had played under a famous college coach, Bud Wilkinson, and then served an apprenticeship under an equally famous coach, Bear Bryant, making it predictable what his teams would stress, James had coached under so many coaches in so many college programs it was much more difficult to guess about his teams. In fact, his first Husky team in 1975 revealed little about the future and the fact James would become the most successful of all modern Husky football coaches. James lost his first game as a Husky coach to Arizona State 35-12 at Tempe. The fifth game was a disaster at Alabama to Bear Bryant 52-0. Yet on the season, his first team not only finished with a winning record, 6-5, but tied for 3rd in the conference and did something no other Husky team had done since 1964: they beat both USC and UCLA in the same season. So if there was some despair, there was also some promise. The last game of the year, the traditional game with Washington State, was a kind of harbinger. With just 3:01 left on the game clock in Husky Stadium and many of the crowd of 57,001 already out of their seats and in the parking lots because it seemed Washington State had a safe 27-14 lead, and making matters worse, they had the ball on the Husky 14 with a 4th down and 1. A first down would have salted the game away for the Cougs, a field goal would have iced it. Even doing nothing except taking a knee would have probably been enough. But Cougar players, perhaps wanting to rub some salt into the wounds of their cross state rivals lobbied coach Jim Sweeney to pass for another score. Wrong decision. Husky back Al Burleson intercepted the ball at the 7 and ran it back 93 yards for a touchdown. Suddenly in the space of a few ticks of the clock it was 27-21 and fans in the parking lot began scrambling back to their seats. Now the Cougars had to run out the clock just to escape with a win of any kind when moments before it seemed there was no way they could lose.

And they couldn't run out the clock. They had to punt to the Huskies and the Huskies began at their own 22 yard line with but 1:56 left in the game. On the first play Husky quarterback Warren Moon threw the ball toward mid-field and a small mob of both Huskies and Cougars. It hit WSU's Tony Heath, and deflected into the hands of Husky speedster Spider Gains who took the muffed interception by Heath and turned it into a 78-yard touchdown pass. Suddenly the score was 28-27 Huskies. Had the Huskies lost and finished 5-6 it would have been hard for anyone to be hopeful about the immediate future and made recruiting a grim task for the new staff. It seems in all things there is an element of luck. That season ending game should have forewarned that Don James was a man with some luck as well as skill.

But at a glance the following season seemed, like Jim Owens' second season, to also have gone backward - if one judged only by the season record and conference standing. In 1976 the Huskies finished 5-6 and slipped to fourth in thc conference. But a closer inspection would reveal that the Huskies scored more points on offense and more importantly gave up fewer on defense. As so often happens in a coach's second season there is a process of winnowing out some players who were recruited by the previous coach and unable to make the transition to the new coach and new program. So the won-loss record suffers.

What was far more discouraging was the Husky faithful were staying away. The home average attendance fell from James' first year of 51,00 to 42,000 his second year. Many were saying James' third year had to be dramatically better in every way. But just the opposite seemed to start the 1977 season. The Huskies after their first 4 games, all non-conference games, were 1-3, having beaten only San Jose State. Then something as unexpected as the dramatic Washington State game of 1975 happened: the Huskies began winning. The first conference game was Oregon and the Huskies destroyed them at Eugene 54-0. Then Stanford in Seattle 45-21. They lost only one conference game 20-12 to UCLA, but because UCLA later was discovered to have used an ineligible player, the Huskies ended up with a perfect conference record and an invitation to play Michigan in the Rose Bowl. Washington, naturally, upset the favored Wolverines 27-20.

Based on those first three seasons one conclusion jumps out from all others: you do not want to play poker with Don James. In the Michigan game, for example one of the key plays in the ball game was a fake 4th down punt. James, in his first three seasons in Seattle, had mediocre talent to compete with, yet he found a way to be successful. After the Rose Bowl, game it was clear that he never again would have to take the field with mediocre talent to compete with. It allowed James to put in place more of his philosophy on offense and defense. In the next seven seasons a Don James Husky team never finished lower than 2nd in the conference. And his 1984 team climbed all the way to the number one position in the nation where it remained in the polls for four weeks.

* * * *

The climb from the bottom to the top made James an object of curiosity to those not merely in Seattle but far from Seattle. But James seemed a study in inscrutability even to those in Seattle. In the first place he became the first Husky coach to coach in a tower. A real tower. Later James would confess it was partly to put distance between himself and others: it was the style of coaching he believed was most effective. It put distance between himself and others. "You want to keep that office desk between you and them. I wouldn't get buddy-buddy with my players." In that he succeeded. One player, Chuck Nelson, summed it up looking backward, "We respected his power and position, his office. We were all afraid of him."

Today Don James has some second thoughts. In an interview with Julie Anne Meisener, in 1997 when he was asked what he considered his weak points, James was reflective without being specific: "I think that maybe I wasn't compassionate enough for players....I care for them and wanted them to know that but I probably didn't do a good job in telling them that...I think maybe I was too tough on the athletes the first few years but I think I mellowed out a little bit." Maybe. But there was always, even to the last day, a feeling of distance between James and the players.

No matter the distance or coolness between head coach and players, no one has ever been as successful as James at Washington and nearly everyone agrees it was because of his organizational ability. Steve Rudman summed up James' style this way:

> "....his system was so structured, so time oriented, so attuned to detail that it made a military operation seem haphazard by comparison. Each practice, each game was painstakingly plotted out, minute-by-minute. There were no surprises, notes were made on everything, all subjects were discussed, everything was reviewed and analyzed. James was so meticulous that when he met the media on Monday mornings

during football season, he had already scripted on a yellow
legal pad every point he intended to make. Seasoned reporters
speculated that James even anticipated all conceivable
questions they might ask, and wrote down his responses."

Clearly Don James was the ultimate organization man. But there
was another side to him that the tower, the coolness, the distance,
obscured that was vital to his success and legacy at Washington.
After an Orange Bowl win over Oklahoma in 1985 and the highest
final ranking in his tenure at Washington the next three years saw
a malaise and decline in the Washington program. A kind of
staleness set in. After the Orange Bowl game there followed a
Freedom Bowl, then an Independence Bowl, and then nothing. For
the first time in years the Huskies were staying home after a 6-5
season in which they barely outscored their opponents 254 points
to 223 points. And they finished not sixth in the nation but sixth
in the conference.

Don James did what a lot of successful coaches wouldn't admit
they had to: he changed his style. In fact, they had lost 5 games
in 1988 but by a total of 15 points so someone could have said it
was nothing more than doing some fine tuning and cosmetic
changes. Instead, James recognized the hard truth that the whole
offense had to be re-created and so he brought in another coach
from the outside to do the surgery, Dennis Gilberston.

The next season, 1989, the Huskies gave up 225 point - but they
scored 332 points and were back in the bowl business with an
overwhelming 34-7 win over a solid Florida Gator team. And it
was the 1989 Huskies that laid the foundation to one of the most
remarkable and talented college teams to ever play, the 1991
Washington Huskies, unbeaten, untied and voted National
Champions. Once again it was a Don James' change that seemed
to help the renaissance. In his conversation with Meisener, James
looked backward at the pivotal 1988 season in which the Huskies
were uninvited to any bowl game. "I really agonized over what I

was going to do and I made a lot of changes in the program, but I also brought the players in more, I think I started listening more in 1988, and I learned that players had a lot to say...I think we got to a much higher level because of the adversity we had in '88 and I think the key thing was to listen to the players."

* * * *

So the dismal 1988 season was truly pivotal to the James' era. Had changes not been made at the highest level then the unbeaten 1991 season would never have followed. Nor would the three straight Rose Bowl appearances of 1990, '91, and '92 have followed. And had not the unbeaten National Championship team of 1991 happened, and the Rose Bowls it is almost certain the sanctions of 1993 which cost James his job and put the entire football program under a cloud would not have taken place. It must be remembered for history's sake that the penalties and sanctions were not given by the NCAA, but the PAC-10 investigated, and on the word of four players who didn't even go to school at Washington, decided there were some recruiting violations. Washington's attorneys had no way of interrogating them. That rankled James to the core because he was obviously a man of high standards and integrity. Everyone agreed had the NCAA investigated the Husky program the penalties would have been minor at best based upon previous standards and rulings by the NCAA. Many believe that is why the PAC-10 held their own inquiry so they could ham string the Husky program more out of retribution than concern for justice.

And that in turn brought about Don James' controversial resignation. Many in Seattle were highly critical of him for not playing through the sanctions and resigning once the team was back on course. Others took James' side and said he had every right to quit a conference that had punished his program so unfairly for such minor infractions. The resignation came on August 23 and these are the words James released to the media after a closed meeting with the team:

"It is with great relief that I can finally make a public statement concerning the investigation of our football program.

"First and foremost, I want to say how pleased, but not surprised that none of our coaches have had any charges leveled against them. They are what I have always known them to be: upright, honest and of the highest integrity.

"I am personally, however, very disappointed that the Pac-10 Conference has seen fit to assess the penalties they have, particularly the bowl ban. Throughout my tenure for the last 19 years, I have worked very hard, and in my opinion successfully, to run a clean program which complies with the letter and the spirit of the conference and the NCAA rules.

"What is particularly disappointing to my staff and me is the impact that this ban will have on the coaches and many of the fine young student-athletes now in the program, especially the seniors. Many of them became Huskies because they believed that in addition to the education and living opportunities that Washington has to offer, our football program provided them with a great chance to participate in postseason play, perhaps even the Rose Bowl. These young innocent student-athletes are being penalized by the alleged conduct of people whom they have never met.

"As for our football coaches, the conference action will also tarnish our reputation in our profession. We have suffered for nearly 10 months from media character assassination. By looking at the penalties, it appears we are all guilty based in large part upon statements of questionable witnesses.

"I hope this experience will prompt the conference to make some changes in the procedures that govern how it investigates and judges future rule allegations. There is a tendency within the NCAA, and rightfully so, when handing out penalties, to punish only the guilty and not the innocent. Hopefully the Compliance Committee was as frustrated and concerned as I was that meaningful opportunity was not provided for them to cross-examine the handful of former players and recruits who apparently provided some information to the conference investigator on which most of the allegations were made...

"Yesterday, this conference elected to add on a second year of bowl bans. However, they will continue to allow us to play on television so that they can reap monetary benefits, as they have been doing because of the outstanding play of our Huskies for many years.

"I have decided that I can no longer coach in a conference that treats its members, it coaches and their players so unfairly. Therefore, effective immediately, I am retiring as the head football coach of the Washington Huskies."

So came to an end the most successful football coach in modern Husky history. He was so much more successful than any other previous Husky coach there was no comparison. The glee and self-righteousness was heard immediately from up and down the Pac-10 conference cities, especially Los Angeles where they take losing hard. But Tom Weir, *USA Today*, seemed to have hit upon the right tone, perhaps because he sat far enough away from the carnage to see it for what it was.

"The Pac-10 is the only college conference that takes NCAA-like actions against its members. And if the violations of a good citizen like Washington had gone to the NCAA, it's virtually certain the Huskies wouldn't have been hit as hard. You would like to think the Pac-10 made an impartial decision, but this was hardly an impartial jury; James' teams, after all, have had a monopoly on the Pac-10's Rose Bowl berths, with three straight appearances. They also had been to bowls 13 of the last 14 years."

When a team becomes too successful on the field, there are often those who seek to do off the field what they are frustrated in being unable to do on the field. I have often thought of the ending to the film *Patton* as portrayed by George C. Scott in regards to Don James. As the end of the film General Patton is shown marching solitary across a Bavarian field with his dog Willie on a leash. Patton recites the words about a returning Roman conqueror and how in his victory parade a slave whispers in his ear that all glory is fleeting. Less than two years before the end of his coaching career, Don James was standing in the White House accepting honors from President George Bush for coaching an undefeated national championship team. He stood at the top of his profession. There were no higher honors to achieve.

James was brought down not by anything that happened on the field, but by things that happen off the field in shadows where men get together to plot. He was never allowed to defend himself by cross examination of the witnesses against him. No doubt he never took the charges seriously enough because he was sure in his own mind he had broken no rules. No doubt General Patton felt the same way once the war was over and the battlefields quiet he was relieved of his command for politically incorrect statements. It is always the political knife in the back that the battlefield conqueror must fear. Don James should have read history more closely.

A good plan executed right now is far better than a perfect plan executed next week.
                    - Gen. George S. Patton

Jim Lambright, a man of mystery.

Chapter 8
Jim Lambright 1993-1998

There are men who should succeed in life not simply because of merit or skill or good fortune, but because they have paid their dues to the organization they dedicated their life to. Jim Lambright gave his life to the University of Washington football program and he did not succeed.

Jim Lambright was named head coach on August 22, 1993 to replace Don James, the most successful Husky football coach in

Washington history. James resigned in protest of the penalties put in place by the Pac-10 Conference and the fact that James felt representatives of Washington did not defend him and the program with enough spine. So one sunny August morning Jim Lambright was brought on center stage. It can be argued forcefully that no previous Husky coach had such an impressive resume for the job.

At the age of 51 Lambright had already been assistant head coach for the last six years and was in his 16th year as defensive coordinator under James. Before that he had coached on Jim Owens' staff for ten years. Before that he had been a player at Washington under Owens. But he wasn't just a player, but a player who overachieved in his senior year. Lambright was recruited to Washington from the city of Everett, a bedroom community about a thirty minute drive north on I-5 from the Washington campus, as a red-headed, freckled, defensive back of five feet ten inches and 175 pounds. And as such for three years he was virtually lost on the UW roster: at his size and foot speed there wasn't much of a chance for him to win a starting spot. For his senior year Lambright filled out to 195 pounds and was shifted to linebacker/defensive end. It was also the first year of the new NCAA rule change bringing back two platoon football. Lambright was clearly a defensive specialist and won a spot on the starting defensive unit. He was so active and aggressive that at the end of the year he was chosen to be on the All-Coast defensive team along with three other Huskies who had the top rushing defense in the nation that year, but only a 6-4 record after being the pre-season favorite to return to Pasadena.

His home town newspaper, the *Everett Herald*, named him Man of the Year in Sports for 1964. The red-headed, freckle faced kid who just one year before had barely enough minutes to win a letter had through grit and determination risen all the way to the top. But there are those in Everett who remembered Lambright as a four sport letter winner in his senior year and who would tell you never to underestimate Lambright. They would say he was always a kind of overachiever long on grit and determination.

Then twenty-five years after his first season as a Husky coach Lambright was handed the torch to lead the way out of the darkest hour of Husky football since 1956, when the Huskies were handed a two year probation. Just as he had been on the playing field, there was nothing timid about Jim Lambright off the field. The *Seattle Times* on August 23, 1993 wrote: "Lambright said the 'inevitable conclusion' about the penalties assessed against the football program was that they reflected a vindictive attitude on the part of the nine other Pac-10 schools. 'The big dog has been shot out of the sky,' Lambright said. 'And the sad thing is there is no major NCAA violation involved.'

The Lambright era began in rough seas, but Lambright, never timid, said the team goal was to win all 11 games and half of the national championship. On paper it was not an unreasonable comment to make as the roster was sprinkled on both sides with players who would later play in the NFL. But an early season 21-12 loss to Ohio State in Columbus destroyed any dreams about a national championship. The next loss, October 16 at UCLA, 39-25, destroyed any hope for going through the conference undefeated and having their revenge on the field for what had happened off the field. The UCLA loss also brought to light a kind of puzzle that was never solved. One UCLA player, receiver J.J. Stokes, almost singled handedly defeated Washington that afternoon in Los Angeles. Stokes caught 10 passes for 190 yards, not a record, but 4 of them were for touchdowns, which was and remains a record for UW opponents. An Associated Press story the next day was headlined: "Stubborn Huskies lose to Stokes and UCLA." Within the story it was revealed how the Husky defense never changed in defending Stokes. Stokes was even quoted that he was amazed as the game wore on that he was receiving the same coverage as he had from the beginning. He said, he was sure they would change, "but they never did so we just kept going back to what worked all afternoon."

Lambright had been a defensive specialist for twenty-five years, and one has to wonder what was going through his mind as he watched one man tear apart his defense and defeat his team? One touchdown pass to Stokes covered 95 yards which is still a record. Being aggressive and stubborn as a player can be a great virtue, but being stubborn as a coach when a tactic is failing can be disastrous for your team. As every successful military commander as well as every successful coach knows, when a battle plan or game plan doesn't work, a change to another plan has to be immediate to avoid a catastrophe. That afternoon in Los Angeles there didn't seem to be any alternative plan for the Huskies. It was live or die with one plan and they died.

A late season loss to Southern Cal 22-17 in Seattle was as perplexing as the UCLA loss. All season Damon Huard had been the starting quarterback, he had some brilliant moments such as in the Cal game when he brought the team back from three touchdowns to win 24-23 at Berkeley and some less than brilliant moments. But he had an NFL quality arm (Huard would later play for the Miami Dolphins.) For the Southern Cal game Lambright decided to give Huard's backup, Eric Bjornson, some playing time. Late in the fourth quarter with the Huskies behind 17-22 and needing a first down desperately, a critical 4th down came up and there was no doubt the Huskies had to go for it. Not only was their best quarterback, Huard not in the game, but the Huskies best runner, Napoleon Kaufman, was standing on the sidelines when Bjornson threw one of the ugliest looking incomplete passes ever seen in Husky Stadium. The crowd was quiet and puzzled. No doubt Southern Cal was also puzzled not to have to face Huard and Kaufman, but more relieved than puzzled. There was no more experimenting with Bjornson at quarterback; next season he became a starter at wide receiver. But on that afternoon in Husky Stadium there must have been countless persons, including players, who felt that they had lost another game they should have won.

Lambright's first team went 7-4, but for the man one player said of, "He's been in the system longer than the system," the day he was named coach, there surfaced unanswered questions which were almost too embarrassing to bring up for those who were hoping that the overachiever from Everett would be as inspiring as a coach as he was as a player. At the end of the first season the idea of winning half of the national title seemed ludicrous for a team that appeared inept at times and without imagination at others.

The 1994 season began on a more rational note and emotions were more focused on the season than revenge for those who had levied penalties against them. There was a tough season opener on the road against Southern Cal. It was also Napoleon Kaufman's senior season, and to get him to play his last year in Seattle and not declare a hardship and drafted into the NFL, Lambright had made a commitment to him to build the team offense around him. The Husky athletic department was also pushing Kaufman as a Heisman trophy candidate, so the opening game in front of the Los Angeles media had added importance, even though Washington was not eligible for the Rose Bowl, or any other bowl. Kaufman had a better than average day, rushing for 152 yards, but the score was almost identical to the last game in Seattle, a 24-17 loss. A fumble here, a fumble there and despite winning the statistical war the game was lost. And once again there were those too embarrassed to ask the questions they might have asked someone else: "What's going on here?"

Just ahead were two difficult games, Ohio State at home and Miami on the road. Both games were televised nationally. In the Ohio State game in Seattle Napoleon Kaufman had a brilliant game rushing for 211 yards and the Huskies won 24-17, although the game wasn't as close as the score. The Huskies then had a bye before traveling to Miami giving them an extra week to prepare for their date in Miami.

The Miami Hurricanes were considered all but unbeatable in

Miami having won a record 58 straight home games. They were coached by another Everett High graduate, Dennis Erickson, who had coached Washington State before going to Miami. So the game 3,000 miles from the little town of Everett had a distinctly Washington flavor. It was played in typically hot and humid Miami weather and everyone expected, including the television crew, that as the game wore on the heat would take its toll on the Washington players, but just the reverse happened. Washington led at the half and then extended their lead by scoring first after the half and to the surprise of everyone, as the game stretched out Miami players had to be helped from the field and Washington seemed to grow stronger. The final score was 38-20, and the players carried Lambright off the field on their shoulders. The Miami side looked shell shocked and disbelieving that someone could come into their stadium and not just beat them, but physically punish them. Lambright and his staff had obviously sold the Huskies the idea that this was to be a take no prisoners game and win, lose, or draw no one was going to out hit or out physical Washington. It worked and became known in the local press as *the Whammy in Miami*. Some even called it one of the greatest wins in Husky football history.

It was also a great relief to everyone who had questions after the 1993 season about Lambright's ability as a head coach. Here was proof on national television that not only was Lambright in control but had perhaps even raised the level of Husky football a notch. The opening Southern Cal loss was forgotten and considered a fluke; the rest of the schedule looked like a piece of cake after *the whammy in Miami*. Washington did roll over the next three opponents, all in Seattle, and arrived in Eugene for their annual grudge match with Oregon.

Oregon coach Rich Brooks had quietly built the Oregon program to a position of respectability, but until they won a conference championship and made it to Pasadena, they were stuck where they were; always a contender never a champion. So in Eugene there was no team they loved to hate half so much as the Washington Huskies. It was their rich neighbors to the north who had been champions all too often and seemed to regard Oregon as only someone on their schedule they were obliged to play. But in 1994 Oregon was playing as if they believed this might be the year they jumped from contender to champion and Pasadena.

The game was televised and the first half seemed a familiar repeat of previous games: Washington dominated. They dominated to the degree that at the half Oregon had but two first downs! Still Washington had but a slender 7 point lead because Huard, trying to throw a sideline pass to Bjornson, had it intercepted and run back to the 12 yard line and on the first play, Oregon called a draw and Washington was in a blitz. Presto, Oregon touchdown. The Oregon score along with another Oregon interception near their goal line, once again a pass to Bjornson near the sideline, kept the score close despite Washington dominance of the game. It stayed that way until the fourth quarter, when a long Oregon touchdown drive, highlighted by several 4th down scrambles by their quarterback, put Oregon ahead for the first time in the game. With about six minutes left Washington forced an Oregon punt and took over with 65 yards to go for a go ahead touchdown. With Napoleon Kaufman on the sidelines or used as a decoy, Damon Huard put on a brilliant display of short passes as he drove the Huskies down the field and ate up the clock until with one minute and thirty-two seconds left Washington had a first down at the Oregon eight yard line. Oregon then called a timeout and Huard came to the sidelines to confer with Lambright and others about what plays to call. On the Oregon side Brooks had called an all out blitz.

What happened next came to be known in Eugene as simply *the Play* and in Seattle became known as the *great give away in Eugene*. Huard passed the ball to the far sideline to his left on an out pattern to Dave Janoski, a five foot ten inch sophomore wide receiver at the goal line. But the ball never got to Janoski because freshman defensive back Kenny Wheaton read the pattern perfectly and stepped in front of Janoski and ran it 97 yards for an Oregon touchdown. A recent story in the (Portland) *Oregonian* read:

> "*The play* remains so revered in the memory of Oregon fans that before each game at Autzen Stadium, a video montage of Oregon highlights is always ended by a replay of Wheaton's interception. Each time, the crowd goes wild, reaching a frenzy that often does not subside until the game is over. 'It's one of the biggest plays in Oregon history,' defensive coordinator Nick Aliotti says. 'You look back then, and to where we are now, and that catapulted the program to where it is today.'"

If *the Play* seemed to define Oregon football, the Washington game did without question give Oregon the inside berth to the Rose Bowl, and they played in Pasadena for the first time in thirty-seven years.

What *the Play* did to define Washington football is unknown. But the critics were heard on the talk radio shows and the stunning loss seemed to unleash Lambright critics who wanted to know why throw a high risk pass the longest route on the field to the end zone when you had two tall receivers in Bjornson and tight end Mark Breuner, both six feet five inches, who a passer could loft safe passes to and if they didn't catch them no one else could. And since you had one minute and a half to score, why pass at all and give Oregon so much time to get down the field to kick a field goal and tie the game? Why not run the ball and kill some clock?

Suddenly *the Whammy in Miami* was overshadowed by *the great give away in Eugene*. It was thought the Miami game was a defining moment in Washington football but it lasted only three games until another defining moment came both to Oregon and Washington football. It's a moment Oregon won't let Washington forget. Despite the Miami win, Washington staggered to another

7-4 season. And there was no longer any polite reluctance to ask, what's going on at Washington?

The 1995 season arrived full of question marks and it was the first time in three years Washington was eligible for a bowl and the conference championship. Lambright made it clear to the local press that Washington had but one goal: to get back to the Rose Bowl. It seemed a realistic goal and there was no talk about winning half a national championship. What there was talk about before the season began was Lambright's decision to change Husky uniforms. He decided to eliminate the traditional gold helmets with the white W on the side for purple helmets and also to drop the traditional black shoes for white shoes. It was not a popular move with fans or players and remains a mystery as to why it was done.

Before winning the conference championship, however, there was a date with Notre Dame in Husky Stadium, the first time since 1949 that the Fighting Irish had played in Seattle. Notre Dame was coached by Lou Holtz, but Holtz was under doctor's orders not to be on the field, so he turned over the sideline to assistant Ron Davies and Holtz climbed into the Husky press box and called plays from there. The game itself had an erie likeness to the Oregon game the year before in Eugene; the Huskies seemed to dominate from the line of scrimmage, but couldn't put enough points on the board to build a comfortable lead. Late in the game with only a few minutes left and Washington clinging to a 21-14 lead, it became clear that if Washington could wedge out a couple more first downs the game clock would expire on Notre Dame. But when they needed them most Washington could not make first downs and had to punt the ball back to Notre Dame. With the clock against them everyone in the stadium knew Notre Dame had no choice but to pass and pass they did right down the field. After a Notre Dame touchdown the question was would they kick for a tie or try for a two point conversion. Holtz called for a two point play from the press box. What happened next was one of the strangest plays ever to unfold in Husky Stadium. Notre Dame flanked their best receiver wide to the left, and everyone expected Ron Paulus, the Notre Dame quarterback, to attempt a pass in that direction. But incredibly the Husky defender left the flanker to follow a man in motion leaving a Notre Dame flanker undefended. And of course Paulus made the easy pass to the wide open man for the two points and Notre Dame suddenly and incredibly led 22-21. The Stadium crowd was stunned into silence not believing what they had witnessed.

But there were still almost two minutes left on the stadium clock and all Washington needed to win was a field goal. Damon Huard had a chance to make everyone forget the Oregon game if he could now find the means to beat Notre Dame. And the moment came when looking for a receiver he saw a gaping hole in the Notre Dame middle and began running toward the Notre Dame goal. He was finally knocked out of bounds at the Notre Dame 32 yard line, and suddenly what had seemed a certain loss looked like a possible Washington victory. Ten or 15 more yards and they would be in a position for a relatively easy field goal. But just as in the Oregon game the year before there was still over a minute on the clock. What was needed was some safe passes or runs. What happened next was uncanny in is likeness to Oregon in Eugene: Huard threw a pass sideline left and a Notre Dame player stepped in front of the Husky receiver and ran it back eighty yards for a Notre Dame touchdown. The final score was also uncanny in its likeness to the Oregon game: 29-21.

It is always easy to be a critic with the advantage of time to look backward. But it is a fact that in the Oregon game the only thing which prevented a rather routine Washington win were the three Huard interceptions, all to the sidelines. It might be that the errors were all the fault of Huard; some quarterbacks under stress look at one receiver from start to finish and signal the defense precisely where the pass is going. But it is also fair to say that is what coaches are paid to do: correct individual problems and not wait until they come at a critical time and cost the team a victory. An incomplete pass in the Oregon game at the eight yard line on first down would have been meaningless, just as an incomplete pass at the Notre Dame 32 yard line on first down would have been meaningless. So the question was bound to be asked: why was the play called in the Notre Dame game that had caused them such grief against Oregon? It was another unanswered question that hung in the air.

In fact, the Notre Dame game dispiriting as it was, changed nothing in so far as the goal of going back to the Rose Bowl and winning the conference championship. And by the end of October and their date with Southern Cal in Seattle, it was clear one of those two teams would represent the conference in Pasadena. Southern Cal had one advantage: since they had not been to the Rose Bowl since 1989, if there was a tie for the conference championship with Washington, they would go. In effect, they could play for a tie while Washington had to play for a win. Washington scored 21 first half points and led at the half 21-0, only to watch Southern Cal score 21 unanswered points in the second half and leave Seattle with a 21-21 tie. As if stunned by failing to win the one game they had to win and blowing a 21 point lead at home, the next week against Oregon they fell behind 21-0, came back, only to lose 24-21. Washington and Southern Cal tied for the conference championship but instead of Pasadena, Washington went to El Paso to play Iowa in the Sun Bowl.

Iowa, which was unranked looked ready to play, but Washington which fumbled the ball the first three times they touched it, looked like a team hung over from one too many tequilas the night before. Iowa cruised 38-18 in Damon Huard's last game as a Husky. With another 7-4-1 season the questions kept coming, what's going on at Washington? There were new uniforms, but the same perplexing games that should have been won that were turned into stinging losses.

The 1996 season brought in two new Husky players who would change the face of Husky football. The first was probably the most publicized player ever to arrive at Washington, quarterback Brock Huard, the brother of Damon. As a prep player at Puyallup, a suburb of Tacoma, he was considered the number one prep quarterback in America, and he was bright being a nearly 4.0 student. Tall and blond and bright he was the new poster boy for Husky football. The other was a junior college transfer from Idaho, but who had grown up in Seattle, a black running back named Corey Dillon. Dillon had a spectacular junior college career, but arrived quietly in the shadow of Huard. Huard was named a starter almost from opening day of fall practice and was the starter when the team opened with a night game at Arizona State. Arizona State was one of the favorites to win the conference, because they had the most talented quarterback returning, senior Jake Plummer. And through a quirk in the schedule had all their difficult games at home. So once again the Huskies were scheduled to open the season against a conference favorite and on the road. On a last gasp drive in the waning seconds of the game, led by Jake Plummer, Arizona State pulled out a 45-42 victory. But Brock Huard had a brilliant debut completing some spectacular passes. Corey Dillon did not start and carried the ball three times. It was the only conference game Washington would lose, but they would finish second as Arizona State would not lose any games at all and arrived in Pasadena unbeaten at 11-0.

Corey Dillon on the other hand became a starter by the third game of the year and was nearly unstoppable as he rushed for 1,555 yards, a new single season record at Washington. But after his record shattering season Dillon made himself eligible for the NFL hardship and moved up to the professional league. For Washington and Lambright it was a great season as they finished at 9-3. There were only two games which left a bad taste in Husky mouths. One was the return match with Notre Dame in South Bend where Washington was overwhelmed 54-20 and

Lambright was quoted afterward as saying, "This is a wake up call to us that we have to get back to Husky football." Translation: too much West Coast passing and not enough old-fashioned smash mouth football. It meant more Corey Dillon and less Brock Huard.

The formula worked until Washington played Colorado in the Holiday Bowl in San Diego. In the first half Dillon carried the ball often and had over a 100 yards rushing. In the 2nd half it became Huard passing and Dillon watching. The result was a 33-21 Colorado win. It was as if Lambright had forgotten how they had gotten to San Diego and won nine games. The name was Corey Dillon.

In 1997 the media chose Washington as one of the top teams in the country and one magazine, *Sports Illustrated*, picked the Huskies to be national champions. So there was little Lambright could do to play down the media hype and keep the focus on winning the conference and getting to Pasadena. The schedule also included a date with perennial national power Nebraska in Seattle in September and some newspapers were speculating before the season began that that game could determine the national championship. On game day Washington was ranked number 2 and Nebraska number 7 in the Associated Press poll. Brock Huard was injured and removed from the game in the first quarter, but his replacement, freshman Marques Tuiasosopo, played well. The problem was Nebraska was a vastly superior team and marched up and down the field at will most of the afternoon on their way to an easy 27-14 win. Huard came back the next week to play, but it was clear he was playing hurt. Then in the eighth game of the year, a home date with Southern Cal, Huard was once again injured along with Corey Dillon's replacement, Rashaan Shehee. The Huskies won the game 27-0, but in the process lost their two most potent offensive players. Washington ended the season by losing their last three games, but it was not because of losing Huard and Shehee. It was because of their defense: in the last three games they surrendered a total of

124 points, an average of 41 points per game.

When NFL draft day came and Washington lead all other schools by having 10 players drafted, eye brows were raised and the unasked question by everyone was, all that talent and so little results, what's going on?

* * * *

The media attention was on Brock Huard for the 1998 season. There was no agreement what to expect of the team except most conceeded it was a rebuilding season after losing so many players to the NFL draft, including two outanding linemen who declared hardship to enter the NFL draft, offensive guard Benji Olson, and center Olin Kreutz. Both had been named first team All-Americans at the end of the '97 season. So there were numerous holes to fill. Still, as the team prepared to open the season with a night game at Arizona State, who were picked to the win the conference and play in Pasadena, the Huskies were ranked 18th in the Associated Press poll. Arizona State was ranked 8th in the preseason poll and was a clear favorite over the Huskies. But in a reversal of roles from their 1996 game when Jake Plummer won the game in the last seconds, Huard completed a 65-yard pass play to tight end Reggie Davis with only 14 seconds left in the game to upset the Sun Devils 42-38. After a 20-10 win over Brigham Young in Seattle, Washington jumped into the number 8 position in the AP poll prior to their journey to Lincoln for their return match with Nebraska. Like their return match with Notre Dame in South Bend in 1996, Washington would have been better off to cancel. The final score was 55-7 and just as the Notre Dame game of '96 did, it exposed the true state of affairs at Washington: no defense.

Before he had become head coach, Jim Lambright as the defensive coordinator, had built a defense along the lines of the Chicago Bears defense which dominated professional football in the late 1980s. The design was to put maximum pressure on the dropback quarterback passer by deploying more people at or near the line of scrimmage. And because the Pac-10 was a conference that exclusively used pro-set offenses and emphasized the passing game, the Lambright defenses were effective. But against running teams which used the quarterback to run option plays and stretch the field wider, Washington's defenses were not merely ineffective but often inept. In fact, the whole Pac-10 Conference proved to be embarrassingly weak whenever they had to play outside the conference against teams which played power football.

At the end of the year Washington defeated a Washington State team which didn't win a single conference game, 16-9, and Lambright was quoted in a post game interview, "Next year we're going to return to traditional Husky football." It would have been better for Washington to have lost the Washington State game because the 6-5 record earned them an invitation to the Oahu Bowl in Honolulu against Air Force, another team which ran the Wishbone offense, which features the quarterback running the option. The losing 45-25 score made it seem the game was closer than it was: Air Force ran at will against the bewildered Husky defense. It was to be Lambright's last game as Husky head coach.

Early in January Athletic Director Barbara Hedges announced Lambright had been terminated and there was a search for a new head coach. The local newspapers speculated that some key alumni had told Hedges that unless Lambright was replaced the donations were going to dry up. Whether it was true or not no one knows. But everyone did agree that the clear favorite to replace Lambright was a former Husky assistant Chris Tormey, who took over the Idaho program in 1995 and quickly rebuilt it to the point where they challenged for the national championship in their division. Right behind Tormey was said to be Gary Pinkel, another former Husky asssistant who had taken the head job at Toledo and built them into a consistent power in their conference. Instead Hedges surprised everyone by announcing she had hired 39-year old Rick Neuheisel from Colorado.

Events had overtaken the time needed for Husky fans to digest them, and there was a shock wave that hung in the air over Husky football.

* * * *

Trying to understand why Jim Lambright did not succeed at the job that he had waited all his life to have is something of an unsolved mystery. He played as a player in a winning system that revolutionized West Coast football to a position of not just respect but dominance. Then he became a coach in the system he played in under Jim Owens. When Don James arrived, he retained Lambright to be his defensive coordinator. On the surface it would seem Lambright had played and coached under two very good coaches and had the chance to play and then coach against the very best minds in his profession. By logical extension then it would seem Jim Lambright had the hands on experience to be as successful as the men he had played under and then coached under. But in human affairs logic all too often has no place. One might as well ask why General George Patton was so successful as a leader of men and others who had graduated from West Point with far superior grades and standing were so mediocre that they never made a blip as Generals in the Second World War.

What is clear when one studies the career of a man like Patton is that he had a plan early in his career, and he believed deeply in that plan and he prepared himself year by year to implement that plan when and if the opportunity came. What Patton believed in was armored warfare and swift mechanized deployment of troops. Patton was a man who believed in plans and timing. He once commented, *"A good plan executed right now is far better than a perfect plan executed next week."* And what is true on the field of combat, turns out to often be true on the field of football.

What Jim Lambright believed in is unclear. No doubt he believed in his defense that he designed and reached a peak with the 1991 National Championship team that was 12-0. So he stayed with that defense even when year by year that defense gave up more points. From its glory year in 1991, when it gave up only

101 points in the regular season to 1998 when it surrendered 298 points in the regular season. It must have been a dismaying thing for Lambright to witness his defense year by year being ravaged, often by ordinary teams.

It is even less clear to know what Lambright believed in on offense. In 1994 he made a clear committment to Napoleon Kaufman to build the offense around him to get Kaufman to stay in Seattle for his senior season and make a run at the Heisman trophy. So the running game was in. In 1995, senior quarterback Damon Huard had 2,415 yards of total offense, second best in Husky history. But running back Rashaan Shehee ran for 15 touchdowns, which at the time was second only to Hugh McElheny's 17 touchdowns in 1951. One could say based upon 1995 that Lambright believed in a balanced offense. However, 1996 was not a year to understand what Lambright believed in. That was the year two exceptional talents arrived at Washington at the same time: Brock Huard, quarterback and Corey Dillon, running back. Huard was rewarded immediately with a starting role after red shirting his freshman year under his brother Damon. What seems a mystery now, Dillon was overlooked and did not get a starting spot until the third game of the year against Arizona. In that game Dillon rushed for 125 yards, then the next week against Stanford he ran for 176 yards, and it was clear to everyone Dillon was an impact player. Had this been recognized earlier, it's possible he could have become the first Husky running back to rush for 2,000 yards in a season. But even in those first two starts, it isn't clear what Lambright was thinking, as several times when it seemed Arizona and Stanford were hanging on the ropes like a prize fighter almost out on his feet and one more good punch would put them out of their agony, but instead of a knockout blowe delivered by Dillon a first down pass was called, an interception followed, which prolonged the agony. The same thing happened in the Oregon game. In fact, statistically from 1995 to 1996 the average rushing jumped from 164.5 yards per game to 219 yards per game thanks to Dillon. But a revealing figure is that in 1995, 299 passes were attempted and in 1996, 290 passes were attempted. So despite Dillon's brilliance, there was no indication Lambright had lost any hunger to pass the ball. Once Dillon removed himself from the scene, perhaps because he sensed a lack of commitment to the running game, the number of pass attempts jumped to 308, and then in Lambright's last year the pass attempts ballooned to 401. Likewise in Lambright's tenure there were three different offensive coordinators. At the end, then no one could say for sure what Jim Lambright believed in.

One thing is sure, the change from traditional Husky uniforms was a public relations gaff of the first order. Certain teams and their uniforms become so entwined with their success that to change them would be unthinkable. The New York Yankee pin stripes come to mind. No one in Oakland is thinking of changing the Oakland Raider uniforms. No one at Alabama or Penn State or Michigan is thinking of changing their uniforms. Blaine Newnham writing in the *Seattle Time* after Neuheisel was named coach and announced a return to the traditional gold helmet wrote:

> "It is preposterous to say Jim Lambright failed because he changed uniforms during his time at Washington, and yet the purple helmet is symbolic of his inability to please either the players or the alumni. Lambright wanted to make his own mark...He wanted to be different. What he was was wrong. He wanted the purple helmet when no one else did. He told the players they would wear white shoes when they wanted to wear black. Tony Piro, the UW equipment manager who has been on the job since 1976 said more than a few players came by after Lambright's ouster to plead again for gold helmets and black shoes. 'It's important to them, they care how they look,' he said."

So what was Lambright thinking about when he trashed the traditional Husky uniforms? It would seem someone who had been so long inside the system would know instinctively not to do it. But once again what Jim Lambright believed in remains a mystery. So the more one studies the Jim Lambright years, the less light there is and the more of an enigma the man himself becomes.

One could, for example, expect someone to come in from another tradition, such as Rick Neuheisel, and change the traditional uniforms, but one would never expect someone who had been a part of the tradition for over thirty years to change them. But as said, in human affairs, there is no logic. The players gave him the nickname of Lambo, a derivitive of Rambo, a popular figure in Sylvester Stalone action films in which the hero mows down villains with automatic weapons as no one ever has - in film or in real life. It was a nickname given out of affection. In fact, Lambright was well liked by almost everyone.

But if there was a film figure to compare Jim Lambright to perhaps it would have been the late Spencer Tracy. Tracy was often paired in films with such glamerous figures as Clark Gable or Jimmy Stewart, and once with Frank Sinatra, when Tracy played a priest. If there was a romantic angle in the film, guess who always got the girl? Not the decent, honest, hard working Tracy, but the more romantic Gable or Stewart. Tracy had to content himself with the role of the hero without the trophy.

For Lambright it was the same. In one season, 1994, he coached his team to what is still considered one of the most spectacular wins in Husky history, *the Whammy in Miami*. Yet only a few games later at Oregon he coached his team to one of the most bitter loses in Husky history, *the Great Give Away in Eugene*. How could any coach and team reach such highs and lows in one season? Husky fans will ask that for years. And it will remain a mystery for only one man knows the answer, Jim Lambright. Lambright will remain in Husky history as the man of mystery.

In the game of life it's a good idea to have a few early loses,
which relieves you of trying to maintain an undefeated season.
- Bill Vaughn

Rick Neuheisel, a former Bruin becomes a Husky.

Chapter 9
Rick Neuheisel 1999-2000

There is so much known about Rick Neuheisel, who replaced Jim Lambright as coach of the Huskies, that it seems there is nothing left to know. He is photogenic, he is glib, and he is a lawyer, in addition to being a football coach. When a reader scans his resume it seems Neuheisel was a man doomed for success.

Rick Neuheisel attended UCLA, but not on a football scholarship. He had to get it the hard way and earn a scholarship via the walkon route. So he did and by the time he was a starter, as a senior, he managed to complete 185 of 267 passes for a glittering .693 completion percentage, which also happens to be a UCLA season record. During his senior year he had a 3.4 grade point average, which placed him on the Academic All Pac-10 team. Not to be forgotten his Bruins played in the Rose Bowl that year against Illinois where Neuheisel completed 21 of 30 passes and was named the game's MVP. Had enough? Well in his senior year of high school at McClintock High School in Tempe, Arizona he was named the most outstanding athlete his senior year after lettering in football, basketball, and baseball. Enough?

It cannot be overlooked that on the way to the Rose Bowl Neuheisel played a key game against the Washington Huskies and in that game he completed 25 of 27 passes which was an NCAA record until 1998. The Bruins won that game 27-24 in Los Angeles.

There is more. After his undergraduate work, Neuheisel was a Bruin assistant coach and found time to study law at Southern Cal and earned his law degree in 1990. He was a Bruin assistant coach until 1993 when he accepted a job at Colorado. One year later he was named head Coach at Colorado. His first two teams each won ten games. Oh, Neuheisel also dabbles in golf and not long ago shot a 76 at the famous and demanding Pebble Beach course.

So what does a man who was named head coach at Colorado at the age of 33 aspire to? Good question. Why did he leave a secure and good job at Boulder to come to Seattle? Good question. For one thing he got a pay raise to come to Seattle, being the first million dollar coach (actually only $997,000) at Washington. And there were plenty of skeptics when he arrived in Seattle as they pointed to the fact that after the two ten win seasons at Colorado, the next two Colorado teams, where most of the players were recruited by him, the Buffalos were only 13-10. But the skeptics in Seattle were silenced when Neuheisel took a team that had finished the year before at 6-6 under Jim Lambright to within a single game of going to the Rose Bowl and finishing at 7-5. And then in his second year Neuheisel did what no past Husky coach has ever done, guided his team to a Rose Bowl, won the Rose Bowl, and finished at 11-1 and number three ranking in the nation. Take that critics!

* * * *

Show me the books he loves and I shall know the man far better than through mortal friends. - S. Weir Mitchell.

But the fact is, despite reading all the Neuheisel biographical data that is churned out by the Washington Athletic Department and turns up in the local press, I am one of those who does not feel I know much about Rick Neuheisel. What I know is what everyone else seems to know: statistics. I could not tell you, for example, which books, if any, Neuheisel would claim to love. I know what everyone knows, a lot about the outside of a man and almost nothing about the inside of the man.

I think one thing is clear, however, that Neuheisel knows more about football than his critics would like to admit. His critics, especially those in Boulder, said he was too involved in playing guitar for his players and doing touchy-feely things rather than getting down to the nitty-gritty thing of figuring out how to beat Nebraska. There is, no doubt, a lot of envy behind the critics because of the fact Neuheisel spent only one year at Boulder before being named head coach. And the fact he has a Southern California beach boy persona rubbed some in the mid-lands the wrong way: you don't beat Nebraska by playing a guitar, they will tell you, you do it with down and dirty smash mouth football. The implication being that Neuheisel didn't like to get dirty or play smash mouth football and thus skipped out of Boulder when the chance came.

But while there is no dominant team like Nebraska in the Pac-10, one thing has become clear from the 2000 season where Oregon and Oregon State both proved to be of top ten caliber, there is far more balance and strength in the Pac-10 than in the Big 12, or any other conference. And once UCLA and Southern Cal regain their status as challengers, the Pac-10 will once again be the strongest conference from top to bottom in America. Clearly then, if Neuheisel continues his success at Washington he will have to be considered one of the best football coaches in America.

Mark Twain once remarked, *"Always do right, this will gratify some people and astonish the rest."* If Rick Neuheisel continues his winning ways at Washington he will gratify Husky fans everywhere and astonish the rest of the football world who thought after the 1993 Pac-10 sanctions that the big dog was dead. Instead they will have an even bigger dog to contend with. Perhaps that was what Neuheisel was alluding to when after the Rose Bowl game he held the Rose Bowl trophy over his head and said to the throng of Huskies, "We're back where we belong, baby."

The cities Europe offers are too full of the din of the past. A practiced ear can make out the flapping of wings, a fluttering of souls. The giddy whirl of centuries of revolutions, of fame can be felt there...Salzburg would be peaceful without Mozart."
Albert Camus, - *The Minotaur*

Harvey Cassill, had big dreams for Husky football.

Chapter 10
Husky Stadium

Every team is known by its stadium. Indeed some cities become known by what has gone on inside their stadiums, such as Rome and the Coliseum. Such as Athens and its sporting fields. And what would the New York Yankees be without Yankee Stadium? What sport fan doesn't know Dempsey-Tunney was at Soldier's Field? *The Long Count* and Chicago are forever wedded. History becomes entwined with cities and stadiums and the people who made the history inside them.

The old Polo Grounds in New York has long been demolished, but what is the first thing any baseball fan thinks of when the Polo Grounds is mentioned? 1951 and Bobby Thompson - the shot heard around the world. If one loved the Brooklyn Dodgers, the Abe Stark sign in right center field in Ebbets Field is unforgett-able, because of the catches the Duke and Furillo made in front of it. The ghosts of stadiums remain with us long after some of them have been at the sad end of a wrecking ball.

Fortunately for college football, unlike professional football, college stadiums remain a living part of the campus. They are often renovated or improved, but never torn down. It seems a friendly place for ghosts of the past to collect and celebrate both triumphs and sweet sorrows. There are many great college stadiums, some of which I have visited, some of them even larger than Husky Stadium. Such as Michigan Stadium in Ann Arbor, which seats over a hundred thousand spectators, but lacks any majesty, because it is carved out of the ground and when you drive by it, very little of it is above the surface to be seen. Out of sight, out of mind. Stadiums shouldn't be built in holes. Like castles, they ought to be admired for their grandeur and history. The Romans had the right idea with the Coliseum. *Aut Caesar, aut nihil.*

The stadium beginning

It wasn't grand in the beginning, because no one thought about Husky football, the university, or Seattle in grand terms. It was built in 1920, like so many other football stadiums out of a hole in the ground. In fact, 230,000 cubic yards of earth were removed by high pressure water excavation. It was designed to seat 30,000 and that was that. It was completed on schedule, November 27, 1920, in time for the Dartmouth-Washington game. In 1936, the stadium was expanded by 10,000 to seat 40,000. And that was thought to be that.

Enter an urbane, natty, chain smoking insurance salesman named Harvey Cassill who became Husky Athletic Director in 1946. Cassill thought like a Roman: let's build something grand or nothing at all. Cassill understood that without a really grand football stadium, Washington would always have a second-rate football program. By 1950, Cassill had put together a package to build a an upper deck on the stadium south side with all 15,000 new seats located between the goal posts. Above the new upper deck was built a cantilevered roof protecting spectators from rain, and a press box was suspended under the roof some 165 feet above the field. It is the highest press box of any American stadium, and over the years many jokes about its height have been coined, such as, "You get a nose bleed up there," or "Even the sea gulls don't come up this high."

The new upper deck became known as *Cassill's Castle*, but it did not elevate the Husky football program into the elite. Cassill hired two football coaches, Howie Odell and John Cherberg, but neither proved successful and Cassill resigned in February, 1956. Cassill never got the Huskies to the Rose Bowl, but he did build something grand; a majestic stadium.

In 1968, Astroturf was installed to replace the natural grass, and at the same time, additional seats were added to the north rim and the eastern end zone, bringing the official capacity to 59,000. And finally the north side upper deck was built in 1987, in time for the '87 football season, bringing the official capacity to 72,500. The outstanding feature of the new upper deck was a glass enclosed reception area called the Don James Center that can be used as an entertainment center on game days or host banquets or related social events. The northern upper deck cost $13 million as compared to Cassill's south upper deck built for $1.7 million and the original stadium cost of $600,000 in 1920.

What is it like to play in Husky Stadium?

It all depends upon who you ask. It's loud for one thing. It's not because of its size, there are fourteen other college stadiums which are larger. And loudness is a trivial fact as all major college stadiums are loud, some merely because the seats are close to the playing field. Husky Stadium is loud not because the seats are close to the field, they are not; it is loud because so many of the seats are above the field and banked down, so that the sound of the fans is funneled by the twins banks down onto the playing area, as one might bank a yodel off a nearby mountain side. So the comfort zone depends upon who you ask. A visiting Army cadet in 1995 said after his experience of playing in the stadium, *"The acoustics here are amazing, a hugh factor. I've been around C-13 transports a lot, and this almost felt like I was on a runway."* A visiting Stanford player remarked:

> *"I've tried to tell my teammates about it. I've said, 'Arizona and USC are nothing compared to Husky Stadium. It's three times as loud.' There's no feeling like coming out of that tunnel and seeing 73,000 people screaming down at you. We've played Oregon, Notre Dame, and Texas, but nothing can prepare you for Washington. You have to experience it."*

Indeed. *Cassill's Castle* remains something unique not only in college football, but in all of sports, something far different than what Cassill imagined he was building in 1950. He wanted something large to boost seating capacity so he could increase revenues and attract the marquee names such as Notre Dame to Seattle. Instead something else was brought about which centers on aesthetics. For example, in the early 1960s at the height of Jim

Owens' success it was thought the support for the Huskies was due merely to the fact Seattle as a large city was without major league sports of any kind. The Huskies, in effect had a monopoly, a captive audience. It was assumed by experts that once major league sports arrived that Washington's fan support would shrink to traditional levels at other colleges and universities set in urban settings such as Los Angeles or San Francisco or Minneapolis or Chicago. But that did not happen. Just the reverse happened after major league sports arrived in Seattle.

The new upper deck was built in 1987 during the Don James regime, and the all-time peak attendance year was 1995, after the Huskies were put on probation! What accounts for this trend that runs counter to other urban schools in America? John Owen, a retired *Seattle Post-Intelligencer* sports writer, posed the same question and mused:

> *"Washington's ability to attract fans in an urban area speaks to the overall tradition, size, and influence of the university. Huskies are everywhere. It speaks to the unique venue and experience that is Husky Stadium, the stroll down from the hill and through the campus, the mountains melting with the horizon, the boats, the lake, the rain, the chill, the thrill of old-fashioned football."*

John Owen tilts toward the aesthetics: the view from the stadium of Lake Washington and the boats, the Cascade Mountains behind Lake Washington, Mt. Rainier as seen from the northern upper deck, the walk through the campus. Mr. Owen mentioned only lightly *tradition*. Gene Stallings, former Alabama coach once remarked, "College football is tradition." Citizens in the Pacific Northwest might be more sensitive about this than in other areas of the United States because of geography. For too long they felt ignored by Eastern provincialism and then California smugness. In truth it created a complex. Their universities were considered inferior to those in the East, their climate made a joke of by Californians, and their culture all but ignored as non-existent by the smart set. If Ring Lardner panned Jersey City at least the smart set knew where Jersey City was; some weren't sure which state Seattle was in.

So, when the Huskies played in Pasadena in 1960 for the first time since 1936, a wound in the civic psyche of many living in Washington was partially healed. And a bond was made, because that overwhelming win over Wisconsin changed the balance of power between Eastern and Western football. A Husky fan even today can still recall where he was on that afternoon and the names of most of the starting lineup for the Huskies.

He can also remember the great plays that happened in Husky Stadium and where they happened. There is no Chesterfield sign to remember as in the Polo Grounds to backdrop a Willie Mays' World Series catch of 1954, but Husky Stadium remains the same. Great players and great plays became cemented in memories by where they happened on the field and thus the field itself has developed a mystique.

As example, during the *Magical Season* of 2000, there was one play that stood out from every other and which will be added to the mystique of Husky Stadium. It was during the Arizona game and the Huskies were stumbling and sleep walking to a defeat. Against Stanford the previous week a defensive back, Curtis Williams, received a spinal cord injury which left him paralysed from the neck down against Stanford. Before the opening of the Arizona game, a one minute silence was observed over the stadium public address to speed Williams' recovery. It seemed to have left the team's mind elsewhere. Then both the starting halfback, Rich Alexis, and his backup, Paul Arnold, went down with injuries. Any loss and the Huskies would be eliminated from the Rose Bowl race. Entering the third quarter the Huskies trailed Arizona and looked flat. Enter third string reserve Willie Hurst, a compact five foot ten inch, 210 pound running back. Mid-way in the third quarter Hurst took a pitch out and broke into the secondary only to be hit from the blind side by an Arizona linebacker with such force the impact literally lifted Hurst off his feet and spun him completely around in a 360 degree arc, and out of instinct he threw out a hand to cushion his impact with the turf, but instead he kept on his feet and sprinted into the end zone. It was one of the greatest balancing acts ever seen in Husky Stadium and the crowd exploded. A few minutes later Hurst once again broke free on a pitch out, this time for 64 yards and a touchdown. But it was the earlier run that will be added to the Husky Stadium mystique. The next week against UCLA Hurst became one in a long line of Husky running backs: he broke his collar bone against UCLA joining another elite list of Huskies. (See Chapter 11 for details.) Hurst's run would have been a great play under any conditions, but it not only saved the game, but the season. It's doubtful Hurst will ever come close to such a display of brilliance again. But no matter he is now part of the mystique of Husky Stadium and years from now, someone will point to that patch of field and remark to another, "I was here the day when Willie Hurst...."

That is what a stadium with mystique can do. Yankee Stadium no doubt does that to a young ballplayer the first time he steps onto its grass. He wants to play better knowing who and what has been there before him. But it works both ways, not merely for the home team. The Huskies in 2000 opened against Idaho, which had 32 players on its roster from Washington state. Many of them naturally hoped to be recruited by Washington and some day to play in the stadium. On the first play of the game, an Idaho halfback named Willie Alderson ran 80 yards for a touchdown, silencing the crowd. Later in the dressing room many of the Idaho players acknowledged they wanted to send a message: they didn't like being passed over. It's like New York's Madison Square Garden used to be the one place a boxer or basketball player wanted to play in to show off his skills. Players in every sport get an extra adrenalin charge in playing where there is mystique. So over the years Husky Stadium has not always been an advantage for the home team: it has super charges the opposition too.

Finally, there is one other aspect to the stadium that endears it to students, alumni, and Husky patrons. It is owned and paid for by the student association and university. In 1959 an idea was floated by an organization called Greater Seattle Inc. to buy the stadium, so they could place a professional football team in Seattle. The idea had all the life of a suggestion to implode Mt. Rainier or divert the Columbia River to California. Contrast that with the professional teams which have since come to Seattle and then one by one threatened the city with abandonment, if the city wouldn't finance them a newer, better stadium. There is the sense Husky Stadium belongs not merely to the city but the state, which in fact it does. One does not need to be living in Seattle to feel connected to it, one does not need to be a student or alumnus either. The coaches and players and various administrators will come and go, but the stadium will remain. Memories will endure.

When the county owned King Dome was imploded in March of 2000, to make way for a new luxury stadium financed by local taxes, there were no protests or tears. Observers accepted it with a detached curiosity; there was no sentiment of anything personal being lost. The unspoken feeling was that the King Dome was merely a collecting point of strangers, strangers who collected pay checks on their way to others teams and cities and stadiums. But those who dressed in a Husky uniform, sweated and toiled on its field, but not for paychecks, left something behind that became personal. If one were to stand in the calm of some evening outside the stadium gates, one might with *a practiced ear make out the flapping of wings and the fluttering of souls*. Salzburg might have Mozart's ghost, Rome its Coliseum, old Heidelberg its schloss, but Seattle has its castle, *Cassill's Castle*, where every autumn in the fading afternoon twilight, legends are made and enlarged upon. That is what makes young men dream and sweat and toil: the chance to become a part of a legend. And what makes it all possible is the stadium. Every team becomes known by its stadium. From Yankee Stadium in the Bronx to an oval stadium in a little town in Indiana called South Bend to Seattle's *Cassill's Castle*, it's all the same; *the giddy whirl of fame can be felt there.* Stop by in the hush of some evening when the lights are out, the scoreboard dark, and the stands are empty and see if it is not so.

Why shouldn't truth be stranger than fiction? Fiction after all, has to make sense.
- Mark Twain

Chapter 11
Made In Hollywood

There are always relationships that do not make sense. Everyone has had the experience of working in an office and finding someone there who brings something negative into the air and you find yourself wanting to be in the next state whenever this person is in the same room. In sports it is understandable when two teams such as the old New York Giants and Brooklyn Dodgers hated each other: no one wants to share the same real estate. Even countries seem to have the same problem when it comes to sharing real estate, such as Germany and France, the Republic of Ireland and Northern Ireland, and Israel and Palestine.

Out West in Los Angeles eyebrows aren't lifted when Southern Cal and UCLA match up in football and make nasty remarks about each others family background before they settle accounts for the territory. The same is true up the coast a few hundred miles when Cal and Stanford square off. Familiarity does breed contempt in sports. But who can explain the football relationship between Washington and UCLA? They are separated by over one thousand miles of the most scenic landscape on earth; plenty of territory to make for peaceful neighbors. What then could account for the bizarre series of events that crop up regularly when they play football, at least since the year 1954.

In 1954 the UCLA Bruins had just come off one of the best seasons any West Coast team ever had; they were unbeaten, untied, and not just the glamour football team of the West Coast but of the nation. Their coach, Henry (Red) Sanders had come west from Vanderbilt in 1948 and installed the single wing offense at Westwood. The Bruins wore gold helmets and serpentined out of the hurdle in Prussian precision. Sanders' system placed a premium on speed and precision over bulk. Watching the Bruins play football was like watching an expert fencer toy with an amateur as the tip of his blade probed here and there in movements almost too fast for the eye. They had rolled over everyone on their 1954 schedule except one team: the Washington Huskies. In Seattle the Bruins had escaped with a 21-20 win. To grasp how bad the 1954 Huskies were one has to consider the raw data. They finished dead last in the conference and lost every remaining game after UCLA and were outscored by 167 points to 34! So there is no logical explanation as to how they could have come within a point of tieing the nation's best team. It could only be explained by the word fluke, or rank overconfidence by the Bruins. Next year in Los Angeles, it would surely be different.

It wasn't. In 1955 the Bruins lost their opening game at Maryland in College Park 7-0, but then breezed over every other opponent as their single wing gathered steam. That is they breezed over every other opponent except one, the Washington Huskies. The Bruins only narrowly escaped 19-17 in the Los Angeles Memorial Coliseum. In the process UCLA lost their most glamorous and important player, Ronnie Knox. Ronnie Knox was the *enfant terrible* of West Coast football. He had originally enrolled at California at Berkeley to play for Pappy Waldorf. Waldorf's teams had dominated West Coast football, at one point running up 30 straight conference wins and going to the Rose Bowl three consecutive times between 1948 and 1951. Knox had a stepfather who appointed himself as an agent for his stepson and decided his future was better in Los Angeles under the new power UCLA. Ronnie Knox transfer caused a lot of hard feelings in Berkeley. In the single wing offense, the quarterback is the tailback who receives a snap from the center in the same fashion as a quarterback does today when in a shotgun formation. Only a single wing tailback had to run from the formation, not just pass. The tailback was the most important player to a single wing team. That afternoon of November 12, 1955, against Washington, Ronnie Knox broke his ankle. There was no hint that it was a dirty or illegal tackle, it just was a freak injury. His injury did not keep UCLA from going to the Rose Bowl and playing against Michigan State, but it did seem to set in motion a bizarre chain of events between the two teams which no one has been able to explain. The rivalry for the next 40 odd years strains all logic. It even has a touch of voodoo.

Red Sanders died in 1956, and UCLA football lost most of its glamour and winning ways. It did not help that, along with Southern Cal and Washington, they were put on probation for recruiting violations. Then Washington emerged as the new West Coast power under Jim Owens. After winning the conference and Rose Bowl in 1959, Washington was an overwhelming favorite to return to Pasadena, because it returned every starting player in its starting lineup, including their All-American quarterback Bob Schloredt. He was to the 1960 Huskies what Ronnie Knox was to the 1955 Bruins. The Bruins and Huskies were to meet in Seattle on October 15. The favored Huskies won 10-8, but one player was injured: Bob Schloredt. He broke his collarbone and was lost for the season. The ghost of Ronnie Knox?

In 1961, there was no clear favorite for the Rose Bowl. Washington had lost every starting player from their Rose Bowl team, except one, end John Meyers, and a winning season for the Huskies seemed remote. By mid-season, UCLA had forged into the conference lead and was marching toward the Rose Bowl with two games left, one of them was against Washington on November 18 in the Los Angeles Coliseum. Washington won 17-13. UCLA did go to the Rose Bowl, despite the blemish.

In 1963 it was Washington's turn to march to the Rose Bowl. After starting slowly in their non-conference games, the Huskies cut a swath through their conference opponents, and with two games to play, it seemed the Huskies would arrive in Pasadena with a perfect conference record. UCLA on the other hand had one of their worst teams in years, the week before they played Washington they had been bombed by Ohio State 42-7. Another blowout loss loomed for UCLA. The Huskies did go to the Rose Bowl, but they lost to UCLA by a shocking 14-0 score.

Tommy Prothro, who had come from Vanderbilt with Red Sanders to UCLA was offered the job at Oregon State in 1955, to rebuild the Beavers football program, and accepted the challenge. Prothro installed the UCLA single wing offense at Corvallis and soon had the Beavers in the Rose Bowl. Prothro was, in a word, a character. He was gruff, chain-smoked cigarettes, used salty language, and loved to play bridge, and by all accounts was an excellent bridge player. He watched from Corvallis as Owens built the Husky program in Seattle to a notch above that of Oregon State and when UCLA asked Prothro to return to Los Angeles and rebuild the UCLA program in 1965 he accepted. By then Prothro had junked the single wing and installed the conventional t-formation and found a quarterback gem, a sophomore named Gary Beban. The Bruins in 1965 were picked to end up in the middle of the conference, but instead became a Cinderella team as they week by week found a way to win games under the direction of sophomore whiz Gary Beban. They were scheduled to meet the Huskies November 6 in the Los Angeles Coliseum. By then the Huskies had been eliminated from the Rose Bowl race, but were a dangerous team because of senior quarterback Todd Hullin and junior end Dave Williams, who was breaking records at hauling in touchdown passes from Hullin. Williams was also a track athlete, an excellent 440 yard high hurdler, who had a long stride and excellent jumping ability, making him difficult to defend one on one.

Prothro, perhaps because he had memories of unpredictable UCLA-Washington games, perhaps because he was a bridge aficionado, was canny enough to take out an "insurance policy" for the Washington game. It was legal, but clearly unethical. Prothro noticed that when Washington was on defense they huddled and no Husky watched the opposition's bench or sideline. So Prothro created a special play where a split end, a player named Zeman, would trot out of the UCLA huddle and stand just inside the sideline, but so close that at a glance he would appear to be out of bounds with hands on hips watching the game.

Dave Williams and Todd Hullin were having a record game, Williams ultimately ended up with ten catches for 257 yards, and three touchdowns, which is still a Washington record. No one for UCLA could defend him. So late in the game with UCLA trailing Prothro called for what came to be known as the Z-streak. Zeman trotted innocently out of the UCLA huddle and stood with hands on hips near the UCLA sideline, but in bounds. Washington's players ignored him and at the snap of the ball Gary Beban loft the ball to Dick Witcher, who had sprinted 15 yards behind any Washington defender for a 37-yard touchdown. Washington was stunned. The Z-streak was the difference and UCLA survived 28-24. And went to the Rose Bowl.

The next season, UCLA was the obvious Rose Bowl favorite with Beban and many other players returning from the team which had completed the Cinderella season by upsetting Michigan State in the Rose Bowl. When they arrived in Seattle on November 5 to play the Huskies, UCLA was unbeaten and ranked number three in the nation. They were naturally a big favorite to defeat a Washington team which had won four games and lost three. There were no Z-steaks and the Bruins lost 16-3.

The next season, 1967, Beban's senior year, it was pay back time in Los Angeles. UCLA was again unbeaten, ranked number four in the nation. The final score was UCLA 48 Washington 0. The next year, naturally, Washington returned the favor and shut out UCLA in Seattle 6-0. UCLA served revenge in 1969 in Los Angeles 57-14.

Sonny Sixkiller and crew welcomed the Bruins to Seattle in

1970, and drubbed the Bruins 61-20.

It would have been natural to assume that when Jim Owens resigned at the end of the 1974 season and Tommy Prothro resigned at the end of the 1978 season to accept the job of Los Angeles Rams head coach, the series would have assumed a sense of normalcy. But it was not to be. When Don James, Owens' replacement, took the Huskies to the Rose Bowl in 1977, the only conference team the Huskies lost to was - naturally - UCLA 20-12.

In 1978, the Huskies were picked to return to the Rose Bowl and opened the season at home in Seattle against UCLA. No one should be surprised at the outcome: UCLA 10 Huskies 8.

In 1979, senior running back Joe Steele broke Hugh McElhenny's career rushing record of 2,449 yards in the opening game against Wyoming. But by the time the Huskies faced UCLA in Los Angeles near Halloween, both teams had fallen out of the Rose Bowl Race. For Steele it would be his last game as a Husky. It was a game that wasn't close, Washington breezed to a 34-14 victory, but Steele received a knee injury ending his career. The ghost of Ronnie Knox?

In 1980, the Huskies won the conference and returned to the Rose Bowl, and luckily didn't play UCLA. But in 1981 the Huskies did play UCLA, and despite returning to the Rose Bowl, lost again to the Bruins 31-0.

In 1983, a walk on quarterback named Rick Neuheisel completed 25 of 27 passes against Washington in Los Angeles to defeat the favored Huskies 27-24, which helped UCLA to the Rose Bowl in place of Washington. Neuheisel became Washington's head coach in 1999.

In the next five games, the two teams split, each winning two and there was one tie. It was like a calm before a storm with one team seemingly waiting to rain on the other's parade. UCLA got their chance in 1990. Washington was having a sensational year, going into the UCLA game near Halloween, the Huskies had lost but one game at Colorado, a game they should have won, and were ranked number two in the nation, with a chance to become number one. The Huskies were lead by senior running back Greg Lewis, who was leading the league in rushing and finished the season with 1,305 yards, a new Husky record. But during the first half against UCLA Lewis injured a leg and was lost for the game after only 12 carries. UCLA once again upset a Washington Rose Bowl team, this time 25-22, and injured star running back, Greg Lewis.

The next season, 1991, Washington went undefeated, but there was no revenge for Washington as the rivals were not scheduled in 1991 and 1992. But they were scheduled in 1993 in Los Angeles, and UCLA won the game 39-25. UCLA end J.J. Stokes had a sensational game by catching ten passes for 197 yards and four touchdowns. Except for the Dave Williams' game in 1965, Stokes game would have been a new record in the UCLA-Washington series.

Washington won the next three games, then UCLA the next two. Enter Rick Neuheisel, former UCLA quarterback as new Husky coach. The 1999 UCLA game was scheduled as the next to last game of the year in Los Angeles and it seemed innocent enough. Washington was picked to end up somewhere in the middle of the conference, but instead behind quarterback Marques Tuiasosopo, was the conference leader after two critical wins over Stanford at home and then Arizona in Tucson. All the Huskies needed to cinch a trip to Pasadena were wins over UCLA and Washington State, the two weakest teams in the conference. In fact, UCLA was having a miserable year. In the three games before playing Washington, they were outscored by the astounding margin of 105-14. But little noticed on the schedule in September was that before playing Washington UCLA had a bye. In effect they had an extra week to prepare. The final score in overtime was UCLA 23, Washington 20. One more time UCLA rained on Washington's Rose Bowl parade.

In 2000, Washington was picked as a Rose Bowl favorite. But by the time UCLA faced the Huskies in Seattle the Bruins had been eliminated from the race and were near the bottom of the conference standings. It seemed a perfect chance to rain once more on Washington's parade, just as they had so often in the past. It seemed history would repeat itself as UCLA jumped to a half time lead on long pass plays to Brian Poli-Dixon. Compounding things, two Husky running backs were knocked out of the game with injuries, starter Rich Alexis, and the hero of the Arizona game the week before, Willie Hurst. Hurst suffered a broken collarbone. Washington rallied to win 36-28, but in the process lost two running backs and going into the last game of the year at Washington State was down to a 4th string back. Once again, thank you UCLA.

Since the Ronnie Knox injury in 1955, no team has caused Washington so much grief by winning so often when Washington was so heavily favored and no team has injured so many outstanding Washington backs. There is no logic to it. UCLA has never had a reputation for dirty players or playing dirty. With the exception of the Z-Streak in 1965, UCLA has played hard but legal football within the rules and ethics.

It seems the kind of thing that only a Hollywood writer could manufacture. But for Huskies like Schloredt, Steele, Lewis, and Hurst, they will remember their dates with UCLA as something like voodoo. And when Halloween draws near, it would be wise for future Husky schedule makers to make sure any team but UCLA is scheduled. Mark Twain would have appreciated the Husky-UCLA relationship: truth is often stranger than fiction, *fiction after all, has to make sense.*

I shall tell you a secret, my friend. Do not wait for the last judgement, it takes place every day.
                                                    - Albert Camus

Chapter 12
2000: A Magical Season

In Division I of college football, because there are no true playoffs, as there are in basketball and baseball, to have one bad game can eliminate a team from having any hope for a national championship. Judgement in effect takes place every Saturday which is another reason why so many teams have begun loading up their schedule with teams that are so weak they are in effect a guaranteed win. There is no rule against that practice. It will continue until there is a true playoff system to find a real champion.

For the major football teams in the West, the Rose Bowl, the oldest and biggest of all college bowl games, remains the Mecca. If a team can survive the season and end up in Pasadena, then the season is considered a great success, and they automatically become part of a great history. It is even better, of course, if they win the Rose Bowl.

Going into the 2000 season the Washington Huskies had been to the Rose Bowl thirteen times. But getting to the Rose Bowl is often a magical journey in that as often as not it does not happen to the best team. The Huskies of 1999 could testify to the fact that they thought they were the best team, but arrived after the season about 110 miles south of the Rose Bowl in San Diego. In 1999, it appeared they would spend New Years Day in Pasadena because the team they had to best, Stanford, they did beat. And the other team they had to beat, Arizona, they did beat. But the team that had no possibility to go to Pasadena and would not qualify for any other bowl, UCLA, they did not beat. That game cost the Huskies the Rose Bowl.

The last judgement does indeed come every Saturday for certain college football teams. One failure can ruin an entire season.

To arrive in a place such as Pasadena requires talent, consistency, and some luck. The 2000 Huskies finished with a record of ten wins, one loss, and no ties. That record on the surface would indicate a great team. But this was not a great team. It was not nearly so good, for example, as the 1990 Husky team which lost two games, but should have been undefeated. Yet it is also true there has never been a Husky team quite like this one.

The Chinese sage, Meng-Tse was once asked, 'If all men are essentially he same, why are there great men and small men?' Meng-Tse answered, *"Great men are men who follow their greater instincts, small men are men who follow their lesser instincts."*

So it seems certain teams succeed because they have some innate ability to follow greater instincts rather than lesser instincts. Very often the soul of such a team is the quarterback, and Washington had in 2000 a quarterback, Marcus Tuiasosopo, with an instinct for greater things rather than lesser things. The team seemed to feed off of his energy from week to week. But even that would not fully explain the nature of this team. One must start with the first game and follow their season from week to week to fully appreciate something approaching the mystical.

Idaho. This was supposed to be the one easy or sure win on the schedule. But it wasn't. The first time Idaho touched the football on the first play Willie Alderson ran it 82 yards for a touchdown. Not a Husky so much as touched him. At the end of the first quarter, the score was Idaho 7, Washington 0. And this was a Husky team which was a co-favorite to go to the Rose Bowl. Gradually Washington overcame Idaho, but it wasn't clean and it wasn't easy and it wasn't pretty. **Final:** Washington 44 Idaho 20.

Miami. The Florida team arrived in Husky Stadium ranked number five in the nation and a solid favorite to defeat the Huskies. It made sense because of the Huskies' sloppy win over Idaho. But in a reversal of form the Huskies were intense and razor sharp in the first half and have a comfortable lead at the half 21-3. But as if playing from a script that required them to make every game close, they revert to form. **Final:** Washington 34, Miami 29. Another ugly win.

Colorado. There was a welcoming committee waiting in Boulder for the Huskies, because many still felt jilted that Husky Coach Rick Neuheisel had left them so unexpectedly in 1999. And those in Boulder felt there was some payback, because the Huskies had beaten Colorado the year before in Seattle. In the first quarter, it appeared Washington might have an easy time as they moved the ball with precision down to the Colorado goal line where running back Paul Arnold fumbled at the goal line and Colorado said thank you and fell on it. Late in the 2nd quarter, Tuiasosopo threw a pass directly at a Colorado player, who said, thank you, and ran it back twenty-eight yards for a touchdown. So instead of being ahead 7-0, the Huskies found themselves behind 7-3 through their own errors. Eventually the Huskies pulled ahead 17-7, and when a Washington lineman stripped the Colorado quarterback of the ball at the Colorado three yard line with but two and a half minutes remaining it seemed the game was over. But Husky defensive lineman Jeremiah Pharms instead of falling on the ball and ending the game decided to pick it up and advance it for a touchdown. Bad idea. Pharms fumbled the ball, Colorado recovered his fumble and then promptly passed for a 65 yard touchdown and the score was suddenly 17-14. Presto a routine win was turned into a nail bitter. **Final:** Washington 17 Colorado 14, but like Idaho it wasn't pretty and a pattern seemed to be set in motion.

Oregon, Unfortunately for the Huskies, the schedule makers arranged for a bye for week number four, when it was ever so obvious that this was a young team that needed playing time to work out the kinks. And unfortunately their next game was at Oregon, a most difficult place to play, because of crowd noise and also because Oregon had an excellent team. It would take a far better performance against Oregon than their performance against Miami to win and unfortunately for the Huskies they played by far their worst game of the year in Eugene. **Final** Oregon 23, Washington 16. The score was much closer than the game.

Oregon State. It was hoped that this was the week the Huskies would put together all the various pieces and play a complete game. The offense, which forgot to show up in Eugene the week before, played superbly against Oregon State, which statistically was the best in the conference in run defense, scoring defense, and turnovers. The Husky defense, however, seemed to be in another state. Both physically and mentally. Time after time the Husky offense would march down the field and give the defense what seemed to be a cushion. And just as promptly the Husky defense would surrender a gargantuan play to allow Oregon State back into the game. Oregon State scored on plays of 43, 48, and 80 yards. Not to mention one play of 98 yards when Washington attempted a two point conversion after a touchdown, fumbled the ball, and Oregon State ran the fumble back 96 for two points! **Final:** Washington 33, Oregon State 30. This is even uglier than any of the other wins.

Arizona State. Week six. Will this finally be the week when both Husky teams showed up and play together? Not if it is night and the game is in Arizona. Unlike the week before against Oregon State, this time the defense shows up and the offense seemed to be in another time zone mentally and physically. Entering the final quarter, Washington led 7-6 but had fumbled the ball five times, thrown an interception and rushed for a grand total of 90 yards. Fortunately Arizona State was equally inept on offense having fumbled six times and also thrown three interceptions. Then freshman back, Rich Alexis, ran for a one-yard touchdown run and another for eighty-six yards to break open the game. The Huskies then added a field goal to make it seem the game was safely out of reach. But not to worry Washington had a punt blocked and Arizona State promptly scored and this is one more nail bitter. **Final:** Washington 21 Arizona State 15. And just when Husky fans thought the team could not win uglier, they win uglier.

California. Surely week seven would be the week when the team would put all the various pieces together on offense and defense. Wrong. California, which had not beaten the Huskies since 1976 seemed determined this was the year to end their losing string against the Huskies. With 12:37 left in the game, the Huskies trailed 24-13 and they looked flat. After a short drive Washington kicked a field goal to close to 24-16 with 10:35 left. Then a Washington pass interception was converted into a Husky touchdown on a pass from Tuiasosopo to Stevens and it was a 24-22 margin. The Huskies converted a two point conversion which would have tied the game but it was called back on a penalty. There was 6:49 left. Not to worry, Cal running back Joe Igber, who had an otherwise outstanding afternoon running for over one hundred yards, fumbled the ball, Washington recovered and Rich Alexis ran sixteen yards for a touchdown; Washington 29, Cal 24 with 6:24 left. On a 4th down punt attempt Cal had it blocked, Washington recovered, and Todd Elstrom promptly caught a touchdown pass. **Final:** Washington 36, California 24. Winning ugly has become honed to an art.

Stanford. Surely week eight is the week the team will finally put together, if not a complete game at least a solid game. No more 4th quarter miracles just a solid game. For three and a half quarters that seemed precisely what the Huskies were intent on doing in Palo Alto as they led 24-6. With only a half a quarter to go this seems like a safe lead. Right? Wrong. Stanford scored and then recovered two straight on side kicks and suddenly with only

47 seconds, the Huskies find they are behind 28-24 with the ball on their own 20. Has *judgement day* arrived at last for the 2000 Huskies? It looked like a judgement day: it rained and drizzled all afternoon, the field was a bog, the ball was slippery, and one Husky, Curtis Williams had to be carried from the field on a stretcher: paralysed in the fourth quarter after making a tackle. His injury seemed like an oman from above that judgement day had arrived. It was - for Stanford. With 17 seconds left in the game Marcus Tuaisosopo scrambled to his right and spotted freshman Justin Robbins alone in the end zone and threw a pass 47 yards for the score. **Final:** Washington 31, Stanford 28. This game seemed to be carrying things too far from the improbable to the impossible.

Arizona. Surely week nine is the week that at last all the pieces will come together. No more 4th quarter miracles. No more fourth quarter on side kicks. Nothing spectacular, just a routine game against a routine team. Wrong. On the first play Arizona completed a 35-yard pass play. A second string Arizona running back, Leo Mills, looks like an All-American running over, around, and through a torpid Husky defense. Trailing in the third quarter, third string back Willie Hurst entered the game and electrified the crowd with two long touchdown runs. That seemed to wake up the Husky defense. **Final:** Washington 35, Arizona 32. It is hard to say this win was any uglier than any of the others. It seems *judgement day* is merely being postponed from week to week.

UCLA. Week ten. Surely this is the week when the whole team will show up and play together. Because surely every Husky remembers the UCLA in 1999 when the Huskies blew the Rose Bowl against this same team. Surely that factor alone ought to bring the sap in the tree up into the limbs - if there is any sap in left the tree. But the hero of the Arizona game, Willie Hurst, suffered a broken collarbone in the first half. Rich Alexis had dislocated his shoulder in the first half. Now the team is down to a 4th string tailback, Braxton Cleman. And entering the final quarter, the Huskies are behind. Which means they have the opponent just where they want them. Cleman played well, including a sparkling one-handed catch of a pass that ignited a late touchdown drive. **Final:** Washington 35, UCLA 28. How long can a team live on the edge before they fall over the edge?

Washington State. Week eleven. Everyone agrees that this will **not** be the game when Washington puts together all the pieces. They must play at Pullman at night, snow is predicted, the Huskies are limping with only their 4th string tailback healthy enough to play. Snow and Pullman bring back memories of other Husky debacles in Pullman and several Seattle newspaper writers openly predict a WSU upset. Washington needs a win and an Oregon loss to get a ticket to Pasadena. Oregon loses to Oregon State and the Huskies play a nearly perfect game in Pullman. **Final:** Washington 51, Washington State 3.

* * * *

So ended a magical season. This was a team which had to come behind five times in the fourth quarter to win games. This was a team which gave up scoring plays of 80, 65, 65, 98, 80, 48, 43. This was a team that everyone agreed played only one good game the whole season and yet won ten times! No one could figure out this team. Their leading rusher for the season, Rich Alexis, was a true freshman and wasn't even mentioned in the pre-season media guide. The best run of the year was made by a third string running back, Willie Hurst. The most critical pass reception was made by a freshman, Justin Robbins.

It was surprising but understandable then that for the Rose Bowl the bookies in Las Vegas made Purdue, which finished 14th in the national polls, and had lost three times, a one point favorite over the Huskies. *Judgement day* was surely at hand in the Rose Bowl.

Chapter 13
Great Husky Victories

Purdue was not a great team, perhaps not much better than an ordinary team. They had an outstanding quarterback, Drew Brees, and some good college receivers. But their record revealed their strength or lack of it: they had lost to several ordinary teams, Michigan State and Penn State, and could, maybe should have, lost several other games. They were ranked number fourteen in the Associated Press poll at the end of the regular season, which seemed about right. A solid, interesting team.

Washington wasn't a great team either. And no one pretended they were, although they were ranked number four at the end of the regular season by the Associated Press. But until the kick off at the Rose Bowl the Las Vegas odds makers made Purdue a point and half favorite. Those in Las Vegas do not quote odds based upon sentiments, it is a business. So it must be assumed they understood something that was missing to the naked eye of others. It was true, for example, that the Big Ten representative to the Rose Bowl had won seven of the last eight games. It is true that since Washington's powerhouse teams between 1990 and 1992, the West Coast had earned a reputation of playing soft football, translation sissy football. So the fact Washington ended up with ten wins as compared to Purdue's eight wins was not a factor. It was not unlike another situation many years before when Washington arrived in Pasadena in 1959 to play Wisconsin. Wisconsin wasn't a great team and Washington had a better record, but Wisconsin was the favorite simply because the Big Ten almost always won, and it was thought West Coast teams played sissy football. Washington changed that with an exclamation point.

But the 2000 Washington Huskies were a far different team than the Husky team of 1959. In 1959 the Huskies were a group which had paid their dues as a unit. No one believed in them, they had to a man suffered losing seasons and played game after game in half empty Husky Stadium when only the curious showed up. In a word they were hungry and as the saying goes, lean and mean.

The 2000 Huskies were unlike the 1959 group because they were a mixture of classes. Remember the 1959 team started 10 juniors. Never had one of the 2000 team played on a losing season as a Husky. Never had one of them played in anything close to a half empty Husky Stadium. And even if they had not played in a Rose Bowl or on a championship team, every day they walked past trophy cases full of photographs and mementoes of the glory days. They knew about the Husky history and tradition. But the program had lost its direction after the PAC-10 probation and sanctions of 1993. Losing Don James as coach, hurt, but it was not such a critical blow as imagined as other programs also changed coaches. Oregon, for example, changed coaches when Rich Brooks left for the NFL and their program actually improved.

It was clear at the end of the 1998 season that the Husky program had lost direction and that was why Rick Neuheisel was brought in. His first act was psychological - but shrewd. Neuheisel returned to the traditional gold helmets and black shoes. He wanted the players to feel they were Huskies by wearing the traditional Husky uniforms.

The next step was to get to a Rose Bowl and restore the idea that they belonged there. The 1999 season almost accomplished that. As a co-favorite to win the conference, the 2000 season would reveal whether Husky football was restored or whether it was illusion. After all, if you couldn't beat a team which had already lost three times then the fact you'd won ten games was an empty statistic.

* * * *

The Rose Bowl game itself wasn't a classic. Washington marched to a first quarter touchdown with the help of four Purdue penalties to take a 7-0 lead. Then on a punt formation the Purdue snapper hiked the ball over the kicker's head and Washington took over at the Purdue 25 yard line. That allowed Washington to have to cover only 25 yards for their next touchdown to take a 14-0 lead. Purdue's offense came alive and scored the next ten points to narrow the margin to 14-10 at half time.

The television crew revealed a statistic: 24 of the previous 27 winning Rose Bowl teams had out rushed their opponent. Win the battle at the line of scrimmage, and you almost certainly will win the game too. Washington's offensive line which averaged over 300 pounds per man, as compared to the Purdue defensive line which averaged but 268 per man. Someone must have mentioned the fact to Washington at the half. The first play from scrimmage of the second half freshman Rich Alexis bolted 55 yards to the Purdue 30. It was his first carry of the game because of a nagging shoulder injury. Three plays later John Anderson kicked a field goal to make it 17-10. Purdue quickly tied the game on three pass plays 17-17. But the trend was set: Washington had decided to run the ball, wear down the smaller team, and chew up the clock. The Huskies took the kickoff from their 33 and primarily running the ball took it deep into Purdue territory and kicked another field goal. And that is how the third quarter ended, Washington 20 Purdue 17. But the trend for the rest of the game was set.

Washington marched methodically from its 45 yard line to another touchdown widening the margin to 27-17. Purdue's offense were mainly witnesses on the bench during the entire third quarter. The Boilermakers gamely tried to get back into the game, but a fumble at the Washington 34 was recovered by the Huskies and Washington ran the ball four straight times for 13, 13, 5, and 7 yards and after a time out ran the ball for 7, 12, 8, and then Willie Hurst ran the final 8 yards to make the score 34-17 with only seven minutes left in the game. It was clear the Purdue defense was fatigued and the game seemed over.

It should have been, but it wasn't. Just as it had all season when the Huskies had a comfortable lead, the defense seemed to relax, just a step or a half step. In football, that is all that is needed between what it a routine tackle and a long run or pass completion, a step or half step. Tackling is after all a question of leverage. If a player is in position and has leverage he makes a tackle, but if a defender is a step or half step slow he must attempt an arm tackle. With just under five minutes to play, a Purdue fullback named Brown ran through several Husky arm tackles to cover 42 yards and suddenly what seemed a safe lead was only 34-24.

After the kickoff, Washington started at their own 17 and on a third and three play Tuiasosopo ran an option play to his left side and found a gaping hole and sprinted up field, crossed the 50 yard line and if he had merely fallen down there the game was over. But on an impulse, Tuiasosopo pitched the ball out toward Husky receiver Todd Elstrom, and Elstrom was so surprised the ball bounced off his chest, and Purdue recovered. Just when the game seemed over a second time, it was not. After a 20 yard pass completion three straight Purdue passes fell incomplete and a Purdue field goal failed. Washington took the ball at their 27 yard line and ran nine straight running plays, including a 4th and 1 play to run out the clock.

The Rose Bowl ended as did so many other Husky victories in 2000, closer than it should have been. One could even say sloppy. One could even say ugly. But it was a great Husky win because had they not won the game, it would have revealed a program still lost in the wilderness and a team without an identity. In 1994 when Washington traveled to Miami to beat them in their own stadium where they had won 58 games in a row, and it seemed they were unbeatable, it confirmed Husky football had not lost its direction or identity. But only four games later after *the Whammy In Miami* came the *Great Give Away In Eugene*. The way in which the Oregon game was lost sent such a shock to every player and every Husky fan that the program never truly recovered. The next year there was the debacle in Seattle against Notre Dame on national television, where once again almost certain victory was frittered away in the closing moments, this time in their own stadium. The next year was the humiliation in South Bend. The next year the much hyped showdown for number one against Nebraska in Seattle turned into another debacle. Then the next year the slaughter in Lincoln made it clear to everyone the Husky program was lost and stuck in the wilderness.

The inability to beat UCLA in 1999 only cemented the idea Husky players were unable to summon mental toughness when it counted. A loser's image dogged them. Had Washington lost the 2001 Rose Bowl game to a rather ordinary Purdue team it might have been impossible for Rick Neuheisel to destroy the loser image that had followed the Huskies since *the Great Give Away in Eugene*. But when the final seconds ticked off the Rose Bowl clock the whimp stigma was gone. Later when Neuheisel held the Rose Bowl trophy high over his head he said with a wide grin as he looked toward the Husky fans and band, *"We're back where we belong baby!"* The crowd's response was instantaneous, every Husky player and fan understood: the exile in the wilderness was over. Huskies old and young everywhere could finally leave the dog house. The Husky band played its signature Tequila, but no one was thinking of El Paso.

Chapter 14
Great Husky Runners

Top Ten Husky Runners 1957-2000

		Net yards
1.	Napoleon Kaufman (1991-1994)	4,041
2.	Joe Steele (1976-1979)	3,091
3.	Greg Lewis (1987-1990)	2,678
4.	Vince Weathersby (1985-1988)	2,653
5.	Robin Earl (1973-1976)	2,351
6.	Jacque Robinson (1981-1984)	2,300
7.	Rashaan Shehee (1994-1997)	2,150
8.	Toussaint Tyler (1977-1980)	1,898
9.	Beno Bryant (1989-1993)	1,741
10.	Junior Coffey (1962-1964)	1,619

If any reader is hoping that I will give an opinion as to who was the best running back in modern Husky history they will be disappointed. In the first place it would be only a wild guess. In the second place there is the problem of comparing two distinct eras: one era was one platoon football and the other two platoon football. One could simply go by statistics and crown the winner as the player who had the most career yards. That would be Napoleon Kaufman who was a Husky from 1991 to 1994. But then what about Corey Dillon who played only one season as a Husky and isn't even ranked among the top ten career Husky runners. Dillon has since his Husky career distinguished himself in the NFL and the 2000 season broke the single game rushing record. So statistics can be misleading as noted by the fact that until 1973 the NCAA restricted freshmen from playing varsity ball. So a great runner like Junior Coffey had but three years to compete. One can see at a glance that Coffey is the only Husky to be ranked among the top ten who had but three years to compete.

And what about a player such as Donnie Moore (1964-65), who competed but two years, but who showed brilliant streaks of running? Obviously there are no shortages of great running backs in modern Husky history and the best one can do is to identify them as to styles and let someone else decide who might have been the best.

* * * *

Speed Merchants: This category would include runners who succeeded with sheer sprinting speed and acceleration. At the top of this list would be Napoleon Kaufman (1991-94) who was said to have 4.2 speed for the 40 yard dash. Once Kaufman broke into the open field, he was seldom caught from behind, one of the few time was the 1994 UCLA game when he ran 79 yards only to be tackled within the 3 yard line. Kaufman has had a successful career with the Oakland Raiders.

Charlie Mitchell (1960-62) was another runner like Kaufman who was a threat to break lose every time he touched the ball, but he lacked the shiftiness of Kaufman. Beno Bryant (1989-93) was another speed merchant with great acceleration and is best remembered for his 1991 games against Nebraska and Southern Cal, both on the road, when he sparked the Huskies to key wins to keep their undefeated season alive. The 1991 team in addition to Bryant and Kaufman also had another speed merchant, Jay Barry, who had a 81 yard touchdown run against Nebraska and also ran for 143 yards and a key forth quarter touchdown run against a very tough Cal team at Berkeley. It would be hard to imagine any college football team who ever had more speed at one position than the 1991 Husky team. Kaufman, who was a true freshman, was listed as third string on the depth chart! There have been numerous other Husky *speed merchants* but none bring back such vivid memories as Kaufman, Mitchell, Bryant, and Barry.

Power: The Huskies have had more than their share of *power* runners, usually at the fullback position where traditionally the big back is positioned. But if one player has defined the *power* runner in Husky Modern history it has to be Corey Dillon (1996). Dillon became the career single game record holder in his only season as a Husky. He was big enough at 220 pounds to play fullback, yet he had the speed to get to the outside on an end sweep. Perhaps the most fearsome sight to a defensive back was Dillon slashing off tackle where he had an option to take the ball up field if the hole was there or swing to the outside where it would be a defensive back or safety's job to bring him down in open field. Dillon had such wonderful upper body strength that he could absorb a high tackle and continue down field unhampered. So he ran through arm tackles at the line of scrimmage time after time, but he was shifty enough and quick enough in open field that he was not an easy target for small backs to bring down one on one. Once beyond the line of scrimmage, Dillon was the ultimate nightmare for a tackler: too big to knock off balance and fast enough to break away. In his one and only season as a Husky, Corey Dillon did not find himself in the starting lineup until the third game of the year. Had he started the first two games his season record of 1,555 yards would have been even higher.

Junior Coffey (1962-64) was almost a carbon copy of Corey Dillon: big enough to play fullback and fast enough to be a halfback. And like Dillon, Junior Coffey was a success from his first game as a sophomore. What plagued Coffey during his career was a foot injury. At the beginning of his junior year, he broke a bone in his foot, came back, and then broke it once again during preparations for the Rose Bowl game against Illinois. Coffey, like Dillon, was an impact player who caused opposing defenses to have to alter their defensive alignment, but every one agrees because of his foot injuries Junior Coffey never came close to reaching his potential as a Husky running back.

Not to be overlooked was Robin Earl (1973-76), a pure power runner of the traditional fullback. Earl was built like a fullback at six foot three and 250 pounds. Without breakaway speed, he still managed a 56 yard run against UCLA in 1974 and ranks number five on the career rushing list for Huskies with 2,351 yards. Earl played several seasons for the Chicago Bears as a tight end.

All around: This category of running back is generally overlooked, because these players do not have the burning speed of a Napoleon Kaufman or Charlie Mitchell nor do they have the bulk and power of a pure fullback so they seldom get the attention of the press or get selected for all star teams. Yet it's also true no team can be successful without them. They have to do the dirty work of blocking for the star, pick up key first downs, act as decoys, in short they have to do many different things well. The most famous of these in modern Husky history was Bob Schloredt (1958-60), who played quarterback on offense and defensive back. The most yards Schloredt ever gained in one game was 111 against Washington State in 1959 and his longest run was 47 yards in the same game, but Schloredt had the uncanny knack of being able to run and pass for critical first downs when his team needed it most, when games were on the line. On defense he hit with the impact of a linebacker and had the speed and instinct to also play the pass well. It's possible he could have played three or four different positions on the team if not at quarterback.

Another great *All Around* back was Ron Medved (1962-64). Despite not having great speed Medved still registered a surprising number of long runs, inclouding a 38-yard run for a touchdown in his last game as a Husky against Washington State in 1965. Medved was selected to play in the East-West Shrine game and played defensive back for the Philadelphia Eagles for several seasons. Other outstanding Husky running backs who did not gain enough yards to be placed on the top ten list, but who were talented enough to play professionally after graduating were: Bo Cornell (1968-70), Rick Feeney (1984-86), Jim Jones (1955-57),

Jeff Jordan (1963-65), Dave Kopay (1961-63), Not to be forgotten is Luther (Hit and Run) Carr, (1955-57), who never hooked on with an NFL team but scored on some of the most dazzling runs ever seen in Husky Stadium.

Chapter 15
Great Husky Passers

Top Ten Husky Passers 1957-2000

		PA	PC	PCT	TD	YDS
1.	Brock Huard (1996-98)	776	422	.544	51	5742
2.	Damon Huard (1992-95)	764	458	.599	34	5692
3.	M. Tuiasosopo (1997-2000)	761	418	.549	31	5501
4.	Sonny Sixkiller (1970-72)	811	385	.475	35	5496
5.	Cary Conklin (1986-89)	747	401	.537	31	4850
6.	Steve Pelleur (1980-83)	755	436	.577	30	4603
7.	Chris Chandler (1984-87)	587	326	.546	32	4161
8.	Mark Brunell (1989-92)	498	259	.521	23	3423
9.	Warren Moon (1975-77)	496	242	.488	19	3277
10.	Tom Flick (1976-80)	418	252	.603	24	3171

No other university team has had such a quantity and quality list of quarterbacks go onto play in the professional ranks for the last two decades as the Washington Huskies. One Husky team, 1992, presently has three Huskies from its roster now playing in the NFL. Marques Tuiasosopo is the latest Husky quarterback to be drafted into the professional ranks (Oakland).

When one program turns out such quality players year after year it is then more than luck. But looking backward, how does one sort out all the outstanding passers and say, "This was the best passer?" There is no way. Statistics help, but do not definitively settle the argument. For example, no former Husky quarterback has had a better professional career than Warren Moon, yet in total yardage he ranks only ninth on the all time modern list. Among active former Husky quarterbacks Mark Brunell, now with the Jacksonville Jaguars, has the best current professional stats, but he ranks only number eight on the Husky career list, just ahead of Moon. It seems obvious then one must distinguish between what a quarterback accomplished while in college and what he did later as a professional.

The position of quarterback by its nature is the most glamorous position on the team, and it requires certain leadership qualities that can't be measured by statistics. Any Husky fan will be able to recall the exploits of such quarterbacks as Bob Schloredt (1958-60) and Bill Douglass (1962-64) who while not being great passers or playing professionally, had the leadership skills to led their teams to the Rose Bowl.   And what about such former quarterbacks as Todd Hullin (1965) who had a wonderful senior season which lead to an invitation to play in the East-West Shrine game in San Francisco, where Hullin threw three touchdown passes and was named Most Valuable Player? Hullin had taken ROTC classes and had a military obligation which prevented any attempt to play professionally after graduation. But anyone who saw Hullin play will recall his extraordinary touch on long balls to receivers. One has to wonder what Hullin would have done if he had played in the Don James era when the passing game was emphasized and a quarterback was expected to throw 25-30 passes a game.

At best it seems to me that if one is a Husky fan all they can do is marvel at their good fortune over the last several decades to have been able to enjoy such great passers and great quarterbacks wear the purple and gold.

The history of war is the history of warriors; few in number, mighty in influence. Alexander, not Macedonia conquered the world. Scipio, not Rome destroyed Carthage. Marlborough, not the allies defeated France. Cromwell, not the roundheads dethroned Charles. Truly in war: 'men are nothing, a man is everything.'

— General George S. Patton

Rick Redman, All-American linebacker, 1962-64.

Chapter 16
Great Husky Defenders 1957-2000

Since Jim Owens arrived in 1957, the heart and soul of Husky football has been the defender. That tradition has continued unbroken: when the Huskies have had outstanding teams, it has been the defenders who have led the way. But when it comes to picking out the great Husky defenders of the modern era it is less clear than picking great Husky offensive players because on defense there are far fewer meaningful statistics. In fact, often a defender will make a key play such as defeating his blocker to ruin a play and another player will then make the tackle and get the credit. Playing defense is all too often a dirty, thankless, and anonymous job. But it is in this area that Huskies have excelled over the years.

Since the 1960 and '61 Rose Bowl teams, defense has been the Husky calling card. On that team it seemed every player was in one way or another an outstanding tackler and defender. Take Bob Schloredt, the All-American quarterback. In 1959 Schloredt was tied with the team lead in pass interceptions with six. Chuck Allen and Roy McKasson at linebacker were deadly tacklers with great range and quickness. Every man on the defensive line was a warrior in the trenches. As a unit their defensive play seemed to make every play a crusade. At the end of the game the opposition was simply exhausted. That began the Husky defensive tradition.

In 1962, a sophomore named Rick Redman, from Seattle's Blanchet High School, started at guard on offense and linebacker on defense. He was named All-Coast as a sophomore and in his junior and senior years was named All-American. Many consider him to be the best linebacker in modern Husky football history.

In 1964, Redman's senior season, the Huskies lead the nation in rushing defense, and that team was the epitome of Husky football. But the 1964 defense, even for that era, was on the small size. Jim Lambright, who earned All Coast honors in '64, weighed in at 195 pounds, Koll Hagen, who also was named All Coast, weighed in at 200, only tackle Jim Norton at six foot four and 240 pounds was large. Norton was the fourth player on the team to be named All Coast. The '64 unit was a killer bee kind of defense with Huskies swarming to the ball and registering stinging tackles. Rick Redman, their leader, was listed at 212 pounds.

In 1966, the tradition continued with defensive end Tom

Greenlee, at six feet and 195 pounds, was named first team All-American. But just like McKasson, Allen, Redman, Lambright, Hagen and other Huskies, Greenlee used speed and quickness to be in position to register bone jarring tackles all over the field.

Al Worley, "the thief," all time Husky interception king.

1968 was the year of "the thief." The thief was a defensive back from Wenatchee named Al Worley. Worley was listed at six feet and 175 pounds, but could have been smaller. What Worley had was an uncanny ability to intercept passes. He still holds two Husky records for pass interceptions, 14 in one season, and 18 in a career. And Worley played only three years. In one game, against Idaho, he intercepted four passes! To watch Worley perform was to watch a master. He seemed much of the time to be just hanging around the potential receiver and often the receiver looked to be wide open, but the moment the quarterback released his pass, Worley had the ability to close the gap and front the receiver and intercept. Worley seemed almost ghost-like.

The tradition of great Husky defensive backs continued after Al Worley with Calvin Jones, (1970-72), Ray Horton, (1979-82), and Dana Hall, (1988-91). Hall was a member of the 1991 undefeated National Championship team and also a number one draft choice of the San Francisco Forty-Niners. Lawyer Malloy, (1993-95), was named first team All-American and drafted by the New England Patriots. Tony Parish, (1994-97), is currently a member of the Chicago Bears.

But no account of great Washington defenders would be complete without mention of some of the great defensive linemen, the players in the trenches with mud in their eye. There was smallish Kurt Gegner of the 1960 & '61 Rose Bowl teams. John Meyers of the same team. Ben Davidson, a reserve behind Meyers who, nevertheless went on to have a fine professional career. Ray Mansfield, (1960-62), who went on to play on the World Champion Pittsburgh Steelers, only as a center, but who was a great Husky defender. Steve Thompson, tackle, (1965-67). Dave Pear, tackle, (1972-74). Ron Holmes, end, (1982-84). All had NFL careers after being Huskies. But there was one Husky defensive lineman who set the standard for every future Husky to shoot at, that was Steve Emtman, (1989-91). To list all of Emtman's honors after his 1991 season on the National Championship team is almost unbelievable: First team All-American Associated Press, United Press, Walter Camp, Football Writers Association, Kodak Coaches, and *Sporting News*. Emtman was the only Husky linemen ever to be awarded the Lombardi Award and Outland Trophy. He was drafted number one overall in the NFL draft by the Indianapolis Colts, but due to knee injuries his professional career never flowered and was cut short.

Without doubt, Emtman is as close to a legend in Husky football as any player who ever wore a Husky uniform. His play inspired all those who played around him and just as General Patton was correct in saying that *Truly in war: 'men are nothing, a man is everything,'* so it is true that in football a defender is everything. For in a football game, where inches are often the difference between a win and a loss, one great tackle inspires the whole defense to play at a higher level. Over the years that is what defined Husky football. No less a Husky rival than former Washington State coach Jim Sweeney on hearing that Jim Owens had resigned summed it up better than anyone has: "You should remember Owens as the man who brought hard-nosed football to the West Coast and gave us all respectability nationally....You never out-hit a Husky."

"The credit belongs to the man who is actually in the arena, whose face is marred by dust and sweat and blood, who knows the great enthusiasms, the great devotions, and spends himself in a worthy cause; who at best, if he wins, knows the thrill of high achievement, and, if he fails, at least fails daring greatly, so that his place shall never be with those cold and timid souls who know neither victory nor defeat."
- Teddy Roosevelt

Koll Hagen, a Husky walkon from Norway.

Chapter 17
Husky Walkons 1957-2000

President Teddy Roosevelt was a kind of walkon in life. As a child he was an asthmatic and restricted to indoor activities. But he was born with a robust spirit and that eventually took him as a young man to the American West, where he became a cowboy in the badlands of North Dakota. But even later in life when he had entered the political arena his attitude remained the same in his approach to life:

> "He was, with all his learning and with all his experience and knowledge of men, still an unusually simple-hearted, and in the deepest sense, unsophisticated boy. Like Peter Pan, he had never grown up. At forty he was applying to the tangled problems of government the ardor, the energy, and the unclouded standards of boyhood. And for that reason the politicians found him utterly baffling."
> Herman Hagedorn, - *A Boy's Life Of Teddy Roosevelt*

A walkon in college football has to have that same unclouded boyish mentality that Teddy Roosevelt had in order to succeed, because all the odds are stacked against them. A walkon to begin with has to put up his own money for tuition and books and board and room at the university or college he attends. He has to understand, in his competition to earn a scholarship, he has to show he is not merely as good as the player across from him but clearly better. He has to understand he will start at the very lowest echelon. At Washington that means starting lower even than the infamous "green weenies." When you talk to former Huskies about their playing days there often comes up, with a smile, a story of the green weenies. In Washington football teams are broken down by color: the first team are the purples, the second team the golds, the third team the reds, and the last team the "green weenies." After that comes the dregs: the walkons. Many Huskies, who later became starters, began as green weenies, but very few ever started as a walkon. Truly the walkon is a very special breed of player and individual.

Even Hollywood understands the value, and the romance, of the walkon. One of the best and most authentic stories of college football made into film is the story of Daniel "Rudy" Ruettiger (*Rudy*) made in 1993. Ruettiger, if you haven't seen the film, was a boy who grew up in a Chicago neighborhood and fell in love with the Notre Dame team down the road in South Bend. Ruettiger, like so many American boys, played high school football. But he continued to dream of someday playing for Notre Dame, despite the fact Ruettiger had the body of a light middleweight. And his grades were something less than Notre Dame required. Despite all these handicaps Ruettiger did manage to attend Notre Dame, became a walkon for the football team, and in his senior year was allowed to dress down for the last game of the year. And was allowed to play the last down of the game - for that he became the only player ever carried off the field at Notre Dame. True story. Millions have loved the film, not merely be-

Two legends of college football: Rudy Ruettiger & Rick Neuheisel

cause it is a true story, but because it captures something within all of us that validates we can, if we have heart enough, capture our dreams in life.

So every college football program likes to tout its walkon program, and indeed the spirit of a school's program is often captured by the numbers and quality of its walkons. It goes without saying that Notre Dame has the most storied football history in America and the film *Rudy* only enhanced the legends already there.

What about Husky walkons? There have been some good ones. Koll Hagen (1962-64), is my personal favorite Husky walkon story because he was an immigrant to America and had played only one year of American high school football when he walked on for the Huskies. By his senior year Gunnar Hagen made the All Coast team as a defensive lineman. It seems to me his story in some ways equals that of Rudy Ruettiger at Notre Dame.

Hugh Millen (1984-85), was a walkon at quarterback and came off the bench to lead the Huskies to their great Orange Bowl win over Oklahoma in 1985. Millen spent several years in the NFL.

John Fiala (1993-96), like Hagen and Millen, was another local boy who wanted to be a Husky and was ignored and walked on anyway, even after being offered a scholarship to play at Southern Cal. He earned a scholarship at linebacker, lettered four years, and at last notice was drawing a paycheck from the Pittsburgh Steelers.

Every college team has walkons every year. They bring something to the practice field that no other players do. They are in the truest sense student athletes. Their desire to play for one team exceeds that of players already recruited and guaranteed a scholarship. Their willingness to start at the bottom, below even the green weenies, defines their boyish enthusiasm to achieve and excel. It is that attitude, if it can be kept alive into adulthood, that produces men like Teddy Roosevelt. And if college football can produce evan one Teddy Roosevelt every generation or so then we will be a richer nation for it.

Chapter 18

The Greatest College Team Ever
1991 Washington Huskies

PERFECTION!

Date	UW	Opponent		Attendance
Sept. 7	42	at Stanford	7	45,273
Sept. 21	36	at Nebraska	21	76,304
Sept. 28	56	Kansas State	3	71,638
Oct. 5	54	Arizona	0	72,495
Oct. 12	48	Toledo	0	72,738
Oct. 19	24	at California	17	74,500
Oct. 26	29	Oregon	7	72,318
Nov. 2	44	Arizona State	16	72,405
Nov. 9	14	at Southern Cal	3	59,320
Nov. 16	58	at Oregon State	6	31,588
Nov. 23	56	Washington State	21	72,581
Jan. 1	34	Michigan (Rose Bowl)	14	103,566
Totals:	**461**		**101**	**824,254**

Co-Captains: Mario Bailey, Brett Collins, Ed Cunningham, Donald Jones.

Arguments persist whenever someone proposes that the 1927 Yankee baseball team was the best baseball team ever. It's the same with basketball and football. And boxing too. Every era seems to produce one team that seems at a glance to have come close to perfection. The 1991 Washington Husky football team thus has its promoters as college football's all-time best team. I am one of those who believe that is so.

In measuring a team, no matter whether baseball, basketball or football, one must first determine where, if any, is there a weakness to exploit. Coaches do this in putting together a game plan before a game. Sometimes after pouring over a film of an opponent they will find what they think is a flaw and from that one flaw build an entire strategy for a game. There have been enough great college football teams over the past 35 years, since the return to two platoon football, that anyone with a television set and a curiosity can recall the great teams from the near great. Near great teams usually have flaws that can be seen with the naked eye. For example, a team might have a terrific running game but their quarterback isn't able to throw with consistency down field. Or they might be terrific on defense against the run but mediocre against a good passing team. And sometimes, because of a weak schedule, a team can go undefeated without ever having to face a team with a good passing game or a good running game. So in trying to determine whether a team is truly great or merely lucky to have a sweetheart schedule, one has to review the quality of opponents too. Being undefeated doesn't always mean more than having a weak schedule.

All these things have to be considered about the 1991 Washington Huskies. Were they truly a great team or did they merely have a weak schedule?

To begin with the 1990 Husky team was very good and could have, perhaps even should have, been unbeaten. They lost an early season game at Colorado after blowing a chance to score with a first down at the Colorado six yard line and then late in the season were upset at home by UCLA 25-22, after losing their leading rusher, Greg Lewis, early in the game due to an injury. So with all their key players returning in 1991, it was no secret the Huskies were thought to be one of the top teams in the country. But a big question mark was quarterback, as the 1990 starter and MVP in the Rose Bowl, Mark Brunell, tore up a knee in spring practice. His replacement was an untested sophomore, Billy Joe Hobart. Hobart had thrown but six passes, completed four for 41 yards in 1990. No matter what other assets a team has when it opens the season with an untested quarterback, there are skeptics. It turned out that Billy Joe Hobart was anything but a weak link. All he did was throw 285 passes, complete 173 for 2,271 yards and 22 touchdowns, for a .607 completion percentage.

But since the Huskies had also lost to graduation their leading rusher and All-American running back Greg Lewis, maybe that was a weak link. Lewis was replaced by Beno Bryant and Jay Barry, two speedsters who were lighter but more dangerous than Lewis. And just behind Bryant and Barry was Freshman Napoleon Kaufman, reputed to be the fastest running back to ever wear a Husky uniform. This combination racked up an average of 230 yards per game. Greg Lewis was hardly missed.

Sophomore Billy Joe Hobart had plenty of speed to throw to down field in All-American receivers Mario Bailey and Orlando McKay. At tight end Aaron Pierce was named first team All-Pac-10. The passing game averaged 240 yards per game. Clearly the 1991 Huskies could beat teams either running or passing the ball. Their offense had almost perfect balance. Oh yes, they averaged 46 points per game, a new Husky record.

But what about defense; maybe there were some flaws on defense? The run defense was in a word overpowering, giving up a stingy 67 yards per game. The line play was lead by Steve Emtman, from Cheney, who was so dominant a college player that he was double teamed on almost every play. The '91 Huskies were so deep and talented at linebacker that they platooned with Chico Fraley, Donald Smith, and Dave Hoffman started, but when Brett Collins, Jamie Fields, and James Clifford came in there was no drop off in talent. What about the secondary? It featured Dana Hall, Tommie Smith, Walter Bailey, and Shane Pahukoa. Hall was a number one draft choice of the San Francisco Forty-Niners and as a group they were solid if not often spectacular. As a whole, the defense led the nation in turnover margin and allowed but 9.7 points a game. Clearly you did not want to try to beat this team by getting in a shoot out, because you couldn't score many points against them.

So where were the weaknesses or flaws to give a team hope of beating the '91 Huskies? One game, the last game of the year against Washington State offered just a ray of hope to someone plotting a way to beat this team. Washington State scored 21 points and racked up a total of 430 yards of offense, 334 of that coming on passes. But there is a caveat here; Washington State had at quarterback six foot five inch Drew Bledsoe, a future number one draft pick of the New England Patriots. Bledsoe was an outstanding college quarterback, but in that 1991 Husky game he was sacked seven times and took some terrible punishment that would have sidelined lesser quarterbacks. And the Huskies scored 56 points. So while the Washington State game provided a ray of hope how to attack the Washington defense, a battered and bruised Drew Bledsoe would have privately admitted that plan wasn't designed for the survival of the quarterback.

To underscore that in the next game, the Rose Bowl against Michigan, the Wolverines had Heisman Trophy winner Desmond Howard at wide receiver and quarterback, Elvis Grbac. Grbac was like Bledsoe, tall and rangy and went on to have a successful career in the NFL, but in the Rose Bowl against the Husky defense he could complete but one pass to Desmond and had a career worst afternoon of only 13 completions out of 26 attempts. So there is some question if even a great passer was the solution to beating the Huskies.

What about schedule: did the '91 Huskies have a sweetheart schedule that made them look better than they were? Quite the opposite. All their most difficult opponents were played on the road, beginning with the opening game at Stanford. Stanford would lose only three games all year, but lost at home to the Huskies 42-7. Next came Nebraska at Lincoln. Nebraska was ranked number nine in the country and had won 20 straight games at home. And although they lost by only 36-21 on the scoreboard, the game was never that close. Washington fumbled early in the game inside their own ten yard line and Nebraska scored. Later in the third quarter a Husky fumbled a punt at the Husky two yard line, Nebraska recovered and scored again. But by the end of the game Washington had racked up 618 yards of total offense and had two touchdowns called back by penalties. In reality this was a blowout of a good team on their home field.

Next in game number six was unbeaten and number seven ranked California, on the road again, at Berkeley. The final score was 24-17, but once again the scoreboard was deceiving as the Huskies had several touchdowns called back because of penalties. Cal coach Bruce Snyder later summed it up, "Against that good ol' football team, a team that motivated and that skilled, you need to play damn near perfect."

And no one could play perfect against this Husky team. If they didn't beat you with the long run, they beat you with the long pass. If that didn't work, then their defense simply shut the other team down and stifled them, as in the game with Southern Cal at Los Angeles when the offense had an off day, but the defense shut down the Trojans in a 14-3 triumph. It prompted Trojan coach Larry Smith to say, "There is no question in my mind that Washington is the best team in the country. They've got a balanced offense, a fantastic defense and they're strong in the kicking game. In my years of experience I haven't seen a better overall team."

After a routine 26-7 Washington win over his outmanned Oregon Ducks, Oregon Coach Rich Brooks backed up Smith's opinion: "I said it before the game that Washington is the best team I've seen in this league ever, and I still stand by that. I thought we made them work for it. The main problem was we couldn't move the football."

So it was in 1991, nobody could figure out a way to beat the Huskies. It was because this truly was a team without a weakness. In baseball, basketball or football it is extremely rare to witness a team without a weakness or flaw. It happens so rarely that when it does happen it seems too good to be true. Thus, in 1991 the Washington Huskies, who were clearly the most superior team in the land, had to share the national championship with the Miami Hurricanes. Miami won the Associated Press poll voted on by the writers by four points and the Huskies swept the other two polls, the CNN/USA Today and the coaches poll, United Press International.

It is of course what happens when you decide a game with votes rather than a real playoff where a game must be won on the field. Despite that, those who were fortunate enough to have witnessed the 1991 Washington Husky football team will be able to recall something nearly perfect, a team without a weakness or a flaw.

Lettermen

Bruce Bailey	Jamal Fountaine	Andy Mason
Mario Bailey	Chico Fraley	Shell Mays
Walter Bailey	Tom Gallagher	Orlando McKay
Damon Barry	Curtis Gaspard	Josh Moore
Jay Barry	Frank Garcia	Jim Nevelle
Eric Bjornson	Dana Hall	Shane Pahukoa
Mark Brunnell	Travis Hanson	Andrew Peterson
Mark Breuner	Billy Joe Hobart	Aaron Pierce
Beno Bryant	Dave Hoffman	Pete Pierson
Hillary Butler	Leif Johnson	Dan Posey
Richie Chambers	Donald Jones	Dante Robinson
James Clifford	Louis Jones	Tyronne Rodgers
Brett Collins	Matt Jones	Kris Rongen
Jason Crabbe	Pete Kaligis	Donovan Schmidt
Ed Cunningham	Nap. Kaufman	Danianke Smith
Mike Derrow	Lincoln Kennedy	Tommie Smith
William Doctor	David Killpatrick	Steve Springstead
Steve Emtman	Joe Kralik	Scott Stuart
D'Marco Farr	Lamar Lyons	Darius Turner
Jaime Fields	Damon Mack	John Werdel

We are here to witness the creation and to abet it. We are here to notice each thing so each thing gets noticed. Together we notice not only each mountain shadow and each stone on the beach but especially, we notice the beautiful faces and complex natures of each other. We are here to bring consciousness to the beauty and power that are around us. We witness our generation and our times. Otherwise, creation would be playing to an empty house.

Annie Dillard, - *Pilgrim At Tinker Creek*

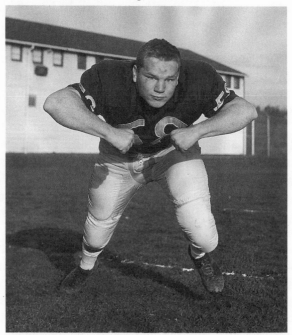

Larry Clanton, the little Husky with a big heart.

Chapter 19
In Memory

As best I have been able, I have tried to compile a list of former Huskies who played between 1957 and 2000 who have passed away. This list was compiled mostly by word of mouth from former players, so it's possible some names have been left off the list.

One realizes, of course, with the passing of time just how complex and mysterious each human life is. No one can comprehend why some lives are cut short, it is one of those mysteries we are asked, indeed compelled, to bare without full understanding. And it seems to be true that some lives are more complex and mysterious than others. But if it is true, and I believe it is, that we are here to witness the creation and to abet it, as Annie Dillard wrote, then it is our duty to witness those who came and went before us. So we witness the coming and going of Huskies.

Some of these men were well-known and had professional football careers after their Husky years, such as Ray Mansfield and John Meyers. Others were not well-known. Some I could not find any relatives of. My best hope is that if we are fortunate enough to get into future editions more information will surface to illuminate the lives of Huskies who have passed away.

Larry Clanton. In 1938 Herman Clanton left Oklahoma to migrate to California, but his pregnant wife delivered their first son, Richard, in Phoenix, Arizona and that is where they settled down. He and his wife had a second son born in Phoenix, Larry J. Clanton in June, 1940 and it wasn't until after the war that they finally arrived in California and settled in the small town of Marysville in Northern California.

Larry grew up wanting to be a pilot or policeman and as a teenager loved working on old cars, such as the black 1949 Chevrolet he loved. He also played fullback for the Marysville High School Indians and was an All-Conference selection and gained the attention of several college football teams, one of which was Washington. Clanton's teenage years sound like something lifted from the film *American Graffiti*. He accepted a scholarship at Washington and was converted into a guard, as so many other fullbacks have been converted at Washington. Clanton was small for a lineman standing only five feet nine inches and weighing 190 pounds. But as his teammates remembered him, "He was scrappy and full of fight." Clanton became a reserve on a Washington team that was deep with talented linemen, but he made two trips to the Rose Bowl with the Huskies in 1960 and '61.

Clanton married in his junior year and because of financial concerns left Washington in his senior year to return to California where he worked as a combination fireman/policeman. He also went to night school at San Jose State and graduated with a degree in education. In 1964, along with his brother Richard, he joined the Air Force to fulfill his boyhood dream of becoming a pilot. He was ultimately sent to Vietnam as a forward air controller flying a small aircraft called a Birddog which was nearly identical to the Cessna airplane. The Birddog carried no armor or weapons. The job of Birddog pilots was to spot enemy forces on the ground so that the air craft with the heavy weapons could take them out. Needless to say the casualty rate for Birddog pilots was the worst of any category of pilots.

Capt. Larry J. Clanton was awarded the Silver Star posthumously for his heroic action on 3 February 1968. Clanton was flying near Long Dien in support of friendly ground forces engaged in clearing that town of enemy forces. Because no armored air craft were available, Capt. Clanton made repeated low passes through heavy automatic weapons fire and fired his marking rockets and destroyed one machine gun position and made it possible for friendly forces to withdraw from a superior size hostile force. That is what Larry Clanton's Silver Star citation reveals.

What it does not reveal is that because of his bravery there are today numerous Americans alive who were able to return home and raise families and go to ball games. His citation also does not reveal that Dann Spear found Clanton's Silver Star citation in a flea market in a California town. In an age when the word hero is too often used for what is less than heroic, Larry Clanton, the little Husky with the big heart, died a true hero on March 23, 1968 in South Vietnam.

Bruce Claridge. Bruce was an end who played from 1956 to 1958 and the brother of Pat Claridge who played for the Huskies from 1958 through 1960. Bruce and Pat came from Vancouver, B.C.

Robert Echols. A reserve lineman who played from 1957-59. Bob came from Hoquiam and was a three time letter winner. He graduated in Mechanical Engineering.

Jaime Fields. A linebacker, Jaime played on the national championship team of 1991 and played in three Rose Bowl games. He later played professionally for the Kansas City Chiefs. Jaime was from Lynnwood, California.

Kurt Gegner. Kurt started all three years he was eligible for the Huskies at tackle from 1958 to 1960 and played on two Rose Bowl teams. Although he graduated from Roosevelt High School in Seattle, Kurt was originally from Germany. After his college football career Kurt was a Marine Corp. officer and served two tours of duty in Vietnam.

Scott Greenwood. Scott played for the Huskies from 1976-78 at tight end and was from Ellensburg.

Glen Kezer. Glen played for the Huskies in 1961 and '62 at both center and end. He came from Inglewood, California.

Ray Mansfield. Ray played for the Huskies from 1960 to 1962 at tackle and center. After his college career he had a successful professional career with the world champion Pittsburgh Steelers. He holds the record for playing in a 186 consecutive games at center for the Steelers. He became something of a legend in Pittsburgh because of his ability to inspire his teammates and his nickname was *The Ranger* for his love of hiking. In fact, Ray died while hiking in the Grand Canyon. Ray came from Kennewick, Washington.

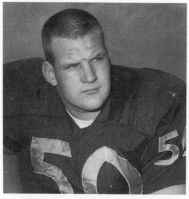

Ray Mansfield   **Roy McKasson**

Don Martin. Don was a punter and played for the Huskies from 1965 to 1967. He was from Lake Washington High School in Redmond.

Roy McKasson. Roy started at center for the Huskies from 1958-60, played in two Rose Bowl games, and made several All-American teams and was an inspiration leader of the team. Roy came from Tacoma where he attended Clover Park High School.

John Meyers. Big John, as he was called, came to Washington to play basketball after playing center on the state champion basketball team of Washington State in 1958, the Richland Bombers. But he was also named first team all-state in football and ultimately concentrated on football at Washington, where he started at end on the Rose Bowl teams of 1960 and 1961. John later played professionally for the Philadelphia Eagles.

John Meyers

Ron Quincy. Ron was a reserve running back on the 1960 and '61 Rose Bowl teams. He graduated from North Central High School in Spokane.

Dick Wetterauer. Dick played for the Huskies from 1963 to 1965. Although he began his Husky career as a defensive back, in his senior year he played defensive guard. Dick was from Seattle and graduated from Shoreline High School.

* * * *

Much more could be written about some of these Huskies. Roy Blount Jr. devoted a full page in *Sports Illustrated* magazine to eulogize Ray Mansfield's life and death, (*The Ranger's Last Call*, S-I November 18, 1996.) and rightfully so: Mansfield lived life with gusto and was always generous with help to anyone who needed it. Some Huskies have passed away quietly in distant places from unknown conditions. And because we are called to witness creation and abet it, I am compelled to witness their lives which came and went but who in the flower of their youth were called *Huskies*.

"Life can only be understood looking backward; but it must be lived forwards."
      - Soren Kierkegaard

Epilogue
From One Generation To Another

You learn, with time, that how you perceive history, whether good or bad, romantic or dull, depends to a large degree on where you were and under what circumstances you lived when the history was being made. That is as true of life in sports as it is of life outside of sports. Since the subject of this book covers the years from 1957 to 2000, it means that almost a half century has passed. I chose to go back no further than 1957 for several reasons. The first reason is that, as a teenager, I became conscious of Husky football at about 1957, and through television, had a chance to witness some of it, which provided me with a living memory of some Husky games and players from 1957 onward. The other reason is that until Jim Owens and his staff arrived from Oklahoma and Texas in 1957, Husky football was lifeless. By that I mean there was no successful tradition to excite a Husky fan. To be a Husky fan before Owens was to resign yourself to always being a challenger, but never a champion. Jim Owens and his crew changed that.

There is some debate about when a boy passes from boyhood to manhood. It is often called coming of age, that moment when a boy leaves boyish impulses and dreams behind for the "adult world." In the autumn of 1959 I was seventeen, about to turn eighteen, but I hadn't crossed the line from boyhood to manhood; I still had boyish impulses. I was a freshman in college and that autumn I saw my first football game in Husky Stadium and Husky football under Jim Owens. I thought both the stadium atmosphere and Husky football were grand. That experience somehow enlarged the city of Seattle in my mind. Then when the Huskies went to the Rose Bowl and won that year, it seemed to me to have enlarged other possibilities in life. It seemed to me if the Huskies could go from eternal challengers to champions, there were other possibilities in life that were open. If I had been twenty-eight instead of eighteen, perhaps it wouldn't have meant so much to me. For by then I would have already been firmly locked into the "adult world" with responsibilities such as marriage, family, and a career. A boy's world would have been far behind me.

* * * *

John F. Kennedy speaking at Hec Edmundson Pavilion

On November 16, 1961, President John F. Kennedy visited the University of Washington to make a speech and help celebrate the 100th anniversary of the founding of the University of Washington. I missed his speech that afternoon in Hec Edmundson Pavilion, which sits cheek by jowl to the football stadium. I can't recall where I was that day or what I was doing, but I wish I had taken a walk down to the pavilion to hear the President speak. After nearly a half of century that seems important now, more important that any football game in Husky Stadium. For while it is true football offers a physical challenge, John Kennedy was offering my entire generation a spiritual challenge. I can see that now, but only after having lived for decades in the adult world. Author Sara Davidson captured the essence of what hearing Kennedy speak was like:

> *"He (Kennedy) looked like and felt like and spoke like someone from another kingdom, and he could inspire the very finest in people. He was someone who could make you sacrifice; he could kindle that flame."*

Perhaps because I had not yet grown to manhood I did not bother to attend the Kennedy speech that afternoon. And perhaps I had not yet acquired the needed maturity so that even if I had attended, Kennedy's words would not have registered inside me to navigate a higher course. For I did not remember much of his Inauguration address, and it wasn't until many years later I understood his words beyond their most general application:

> *I do not believe that any of us would exchange places with any other people or any other generation. The energy, the faith, the devotion which we bring to this endeavor will light our country and all who serve it - and the glow from that fire can truly light the world."*
> John F. Kennedy, - Inauguration Address, 1961

But I was quite sure of some things at eighteen, one was that I would someday become a football or basketball coach and high school teacher. I also thought I would do that in Seattle, because I thought Seattle was all that any person could want as a city to live in. But the adult world got in the way of boyish impulses. Soon came time spent in the U.S. Army and time spent in places overseas, such as West Germany, and then Vietnam. I suppose that was what John Kennedy was trying to tell us in his Inauguration speech, but few of us were really paying attention - at eighteen. Many years later when we took the time to read his speeches we understood the meaning of his challenge to us: go out into the world and carry the torch of freedom to it.

I did become a high school teacher and basketball coach for a period. But what I gave myself up to in life was to be a writer, because after Kennedy's death and my experience in the military, I thought writing was one possibility of fulfilling the challenge of helping freedom in the world. And as I progressed beyond boyhood to adulthood, I came to have less faith in guns than I did in the power of ideas.

But with the passing of time, I understood that the Greeks were onto something when they played games. There is something that changes the core of a person when he submits himself to training for a sport that demands sacrifice of the individual for the experience of living something larger. For after that the individual is never quite the same person again. The Greeks intuitively knew that, or discovered it, and required of their youth a regiment in sports. So no matter how far I journeyed from boyhood I could never escape the influence of sports.

It is why, I suppose, when I look back at my years as a student in the early '60s, and memories of Seattle, it looks terribly romantic and better than it looks today. Seattle, for instance has changed profoundly. I recently read a scathing review of Seattle, by a writer who once lived in Seattle and moved to, of all places, Los Angeles. He wrote:

> "Through much of the '80s and the first half of the '90s, Seattle believed its press clippings. *The Most Livable* of American cities - and I lived there during that era...It was a quaint idea, and wholly realized for a while. 'We're not going to make the same mistakes as L.A.,' I would hear, repetitively. Of course Seattle made all of them, and then

some...Ordinary neighborhoods became exclusive. Teachers, nurses, and fishmongers are forced into cars for long commutes to the suburbs to accommodate families."
    - John Balzar, *Los Angeles Times*, April, 2001

At first glance I thought Mr. Balzar was overly harsh in his criticism, perhaps the venting of a rejected lover. But then, with a smile, I realized he was more right than wrong. Seattle grew up, as everyone and every city must. Who could ever imagine there would be such great sky scrappers in downtown Seattle - or such L.A. like traffic jams. In the adult world change is inevitable and no one can predict with certainty what people or places will grow up to be like. Seattle didn't turn out to be the place where I wanted to live forever. It was just another a boyish illusion.

The Hasty Tasty on University Ave. NE (circa 1960).

Just as Seattle has changed, so has the University of Washington. Like its football stadium, the university has gotten larger. And like

Seattle, it seems less friendly, more in a rush, more preoccupied with its image. And that has spilled over to the neighborhoods surrounding the university itself. There used to be student hangouts and dives such as the Century Tavern and the Hasty Tasty, an all-night greasy spoon, on University Avenue that became institutions. They have long since vanished for more upscale places, of course it takes a good deal more money to be a student at any large university today, and such places as the Century Tavern and Hasty Tasty are no longer needed or missed by those who can afford to study at the university. But those places gave the university itself a certain flavor that has vanished.

* * * *

By my count, I found there were 955 young men who managed to become lettermen in football at the University of Washington from 1957 to 2000. That is less than what I'd guessed there would have been by a few hundred. But that does not include all those hardy young men who managed, like Rudy Ruettiger at Notre Dame, to survive the rigors for one season or more as non-lettermen and who never played in a game. To my way of thinking, those who didn't letter are as much a part of Husky history as any of the stars, although unlike Rudy Ruettiger, no movies have been made about them, and they have gone on to their jobs in life anonymously.

What is known about those sturdy young men who came to the University of Washington to play football is that later in life they became doctors, lawyers, teachers, businessmen, truck drivers, salesmen, construction managers and workers, policemen, politicians, including one who became a career Congressman, and not a few became football coaches themselves. There have been a few scofflaws that I know of, but which you will not find in this book. One former Husky actually managed to spend some time in the state prison. Another, Bob Jarvis, lost both legs in a construction accident, and the Bob Jarvis Award given each year is named after him.

I was curious as to whether I would find a Husky who had chosen my profession of writing. I have not, but it does not mean one of them has not done so because as I have said, like other Americans, many Huskies have moved to distant places far from Seattle.

It has brought to mind a passage that I read years ago when I was serving my apprenticeship as a writer from a small book, *The Unquiet Grave*, by British critic, Cyril Connolly:

> *As we grow older, in fact, we discover that the lives of most human beings are worthless except in so far as they contribute to the enrichment and emancipation of the spirit. However attractive in our youth animal graces may be, if in our maturity they have not led us to emend our character in the corrupt text of existence, then our time has been wasted. No one over thirty-five is worth meeting who has not something to teach us, - something more than we could learn from a book.*

I can see now that my thirty-fifth year has long since faded in the rear view mirror that thirty-five is a kind of watershed point in life where one ought to have taken measure of what time means in the context of a life. Each of us has just so much time in life to fulfill that which we have chosen to do. The problem is that none of us knows how much time we are allotted. So I have spent more time in this book in examining the lives of those Huskies over the age of thirty-five than those under thirty-five.

Gunnar Koll Hagen

I have interviewed only a small fraction of the men who played and coached football at Washington. But even at that there is one former player who seems in my mind to stand out from the others who played football at Washington. He still lives in Seattle. He never made any All-American team, although after his senior year he was selected to the All-Coast team. There seems nothing special

Koll Hagen Husky 1964   **Koll Hagen businessman 2001**

about him until you sit down with him over a cup of coffee and talk about life.

Gunnar Koll Hagen grew up in a village outside Oslo, Norway. At the age of twelve he immigrated to the United State with his family, and after stops in Canada and Southern California they settled in the Ballard section of Seattle. He spoke little English. What Koll liked to do as a teenager was swim and ski. But by the time he was a senior at Ballard High School, it became clear that if he had any hopes of continuing his education beyond high school, he would need some kind of scholarship, and there were none in swimming or skiing. Someone suggested American football, which Koll had never played before. So Koll went out for the Ballard Beaver team, made it, and was named to the Seattle All-Metro team. But there was no offer of a scholarship from anyone, so Koll did the only thing he could. One August afternoon he walked into the office of Chesty Walker at the University of Washington and asked for permission to go out for the football team.

It wasn't long after that that Koll Hagen had a scholarship. Like a lot of the Huskies he wasn't big, but somewhat undersized for college football at six foot and 200 pounds. What he didn't lack was quickness and lots of heart. He played alongside another Husky who was undersized, but was quick with lots of heart, Jim Lambright. Both were selected to the All-Coast team in 1964. There were no professional offers for Koll, and after college he ended up in the Marine Corp and in Vietnam where he was a platoon leader.

When I asked Hagen if he ever had any doubts that he'd get out of Vietnam in one piece and back to Ballard, he merely smiled a Huck Finnish grin, as if not understanding the question. "No," he answered, as if to humor me for asking such a silly question, "I always figured I would find a way to get home in one piece. There was never any doubt in my mind."

I understood then there was probably never any doubt that somehow he would also earn his scholarship at Washington. Doubt is something foreign to the thinking of Koll Hagen. So is the idea of not having fun in life. He remembers fondly a time in Los Angeles after a football game, and the team had an evening to kill before their flight home to Seattle. There was a curfew, but one of the Huskies knew some girls in Los Angeles, and urged Koll to come with him in violation of the team curfew. Koll made the decision to go. As he explained, "I played as hard as I could during the game, but I saw no reason to suffer after the game. That doesn't make sense to me."

What seems to come across about Koll Hagen's view of life and living is balance. When there is work to do, he rolls up his sleeves and goes at it full bore. But when the work is over, then, if it is possible to enjoy life, he tries to enjoy it full bore too. He explains he enjoyed every minute of being a Husky and regrets nothing. His teammates remember him the same way: mention the name of Gunnar Koll Hagen, and a smile will instantly spread across the face of the former player. To me that is the highest compliment a former comrade can give another. It is the surest sign that his memory generates warmth and good will.

I suppose the reason Gunnar Koll Hagen stands out from the Huskies I've interviewed is the fact that he seems to me more than any other to have made the most of what he had a chance to do. Hagen answered the challenge both when he was in college and after he was out of college. He did not, for example, have to be a Marine, but chose to be one. He could have probably found a way to avoid Vietnam, but instead became a Marine which almost guaranteed him time there.

College Football Today

So much, it seems, has changed since I was a student forty odd years ago. Like Seattle, like the university, like life itself, today everything seems to revolve around money. A college football coach today makes more money than we could have dreamed of a generation ago. But so do players who leave college football for the professional league. Today everything seems on a scale that we could not imagine. A college football coach today is thrown into this atmosphere where winning is everything because it is only through winning that money is produced. At Washington it is football that pays the bills for all other sports for men and women for no other sport generates revenue. It is the same at other universities.

Rick Telander, a former *Sports Illustrated* writer and a graduate of Northwestern University, wrote in his book *The Hundred Yard Lie*:

> *"As a group, college football coaches are not brilliant or even reflective men. But they are almost all cunning, clever, savvy, hardworking, dedicated, practical, and to varying degrees, sincere. But high intelligence can burden a coach the way a fine sense of smell can burden a sewer worker."*

Telander's book, published in 1990, is a 223 page diatribe that catalogues all the ills and warts of college football. He did not invent these ills and warts, they were and are still real. Everyone knows they exist. But it was not my purpose in this book to point them out nor is it my purpose to pretend they do not exist. I have spent so little time in this book on the problems of college football, because I believe for all of its problems, college athletics, including football, produces more good than bad.

Today the college football coach has little time to find balance in his personal life or to seek players who bring balance with them to the school, like the Koll Hagens. So my sympathies, with a few exceptions, are with the coaches who are fighting this constant pressure to win and keep the money coming in.

I would like to think college football would reform itself, just as I would like to think the American political system would reform itself. But we see how that struggle goes on from decade to decade and then generation to generation. We see how addictive money is and how it corrupts everything it touches.

So it is today in college football. It was not so long ago a game for student-athletes, and now it is a game for semi-professionals who spend some time at a university, but seldom graduate, then audition for professional teams. The connection between player and school becomes remote and artificial. It has to do with money. Looking backward now to the Washington Rose Bowl team of 1960, in which every starting player ultimately graduated with a degree, four of them with degrees in Engineering, I see how much things have changed in one generation. Trying to project forward to the next generation and imagine the future of college football seems bleak.

While it seems remote that college football will reform itself and get back to true student-athletes, one can always, and must, hope.

Football: A True American Game

"General Patton, was convinced that character is bestowed by nature; that there are certain and permanent character traits; and that people do things exactly as they are constituted - Americans in their fashion and the British in their own ingrained ways."
Ladislas Farago, - *Patton: Ordeal and Triumph*

I can see now, with the passing of time, how truly American

football is. That understanding has come about because I have spent so much time working abroad, mostly in Europe, where as in other places around the globe the game of soccer is taken with a religious fervor. Yet that fervor has escaped me, as it has millions of other Americans, and I have given much thought as to why. It seems every few years some promoter of soccer, following an international tournament where an American stadium was sold out, such as the Rose Bowl in Pasadena, in a bubble of enthusiasm will exclaim, "Ah, the Yanks have matured to the point where they now understand and appreciate the game of soccer." And a new professional league is organized.

But the television ratings for subsequent professional soccer are always dismal, the attendance mediocre, barely enough to breathe life into the financial coffers. Last summer in the Czech Republic I accepted an invitation to watch on television the EuroCup 2000 at the home of a friend. And as I watched, the question pricked at me all over again: why was I left cold watching the contest between the Czech National team and the French National team? To be honest the footwork of the players was dazzling.

But as the game wore on to another of those dreary low scoring 1-0 finishes or 1-1 stalemates, which require a shootout, I noticed how often the ball was kicked backward, or even out of bounds, as a strategy and how on the great bulk of the playing field nothing of interest happened, because it was impossible to score unless the ball was within a few yards of the goal.

Contrast that to American football, which is a lineal game, and where a team never goes backward unless from a penalty or a lousy play. Even if the ball is ninety-five yards from the goal the offensive team has the potential to score a touchdown through a pass or run. It happens just often enough that it sustains the tension and interest in the contest at all times. In other words there are no dead spots on an American football field.

In the classic film *Patton*, starring George C. Scott as General Patton, the film opened with what is now the most famous opening speech in film history, the speech General Patton delivered to his troops where he said, "Men, I don't want to receive any reports that we're holding our ground. We aren't holding anything. We're going straight ahead. Let the hun hold his ground. We're going to go through those Huns like crap through a goose!"

General Patton is often used as an example of what a perfect football coach should be, because he used salty and profane language in his speeches. But that aside what is remarkable about that Patton speech is how brilliantly he captured the American psychology about warfare: you went straight ahead, captured enemy ground, always pushing the enemy backward - just as in American football.

So the American man is different from his French or British or Italian counterpart. The psychology is different in American sports as well as life. Quite to the contrary then the lack of fervor for soccer in America comes not because Americans don't understand it, but rather because they do understand it and prefer something else which is closer to the American character.

What cannot be denied is that the human anatomy wasn't designed for American football, especially the joints. The most basic acts in American football put players at risk of injury on every play, despite the amount of protective gear worn. There is a recent movement toward a return to playing on natural grass to try and cut down on the injuries to knees and ankles, but I doubt it will significantly cut down on those injuries, because driving a shoulder into another player's legs either on a tackle or a block violates the design of the human anatomy. Despite that obvious fact to one and all, I do not imagine that young American boys will turn away from American football. Once again it is a question of psychology; there is something about the sight of robust young men in uniforms driving in unison toward a goal and on the other side young men trying mightily to deny that forward movement, that stimulates admiration in Americans. I do not see that as changing. It seems to have taken root in our national psychology. It explains the passion of a Rudy Ruettiger, who came from a family of emigrants in Chicago, to attend a university, Notre

Dame, which he had never seen and which he had so little real chance to ever attend let alone play football for. Ruettiger knew the history of Knute Rockne and the speech of the Gipper as if they had existed in his own time.

There was a popular Husky lapel button not long ago worn by Washington Husky fans which read, *"On the eighth day God made Huskies."* There was a touch of humor in it, but it was at the same time a slice of provincialism that infects us all. I believe it has always been with us, and we shall not escape it no matter how sophisticated or worldly we become on the exterior.

It means that some of us shall always be Huskies. *Once a Husky, always a Husky.* I suppose I am doomed to be one of them.

Part II

WASHINGTON LETTERMEN 1957 - 2000

A

Aguirre, Dick 1959, 60
Akina, Duane 1976-78
Albritton Vince 1981
Aleaga, Ink 1994-96
Albrecht, Ben 1970-72
Alkire, Andy 1960-62
Allen, Anthony 1979, 80, 81
Allen, Cal 1969
Allen, Chuck 1958-60
Allen, John 1983, 84
Allen, Mike 1987, 88
Alozie, Eric 1988
Alvarado, Tony 1980, 81
Ames, Bill 1986-87
Anderson, Bob 1966-68
Anderson, Jim 1973, 74
Anderson, James 1975
Anderson, Steve 1971
Andre, Phil 1971, 72
Andres, Ricky 1985-88
Andrilenas, Jim 1971, 73
Apostle, Tony 1971
Armstrong, Don 1956-58
Arnold, Paul 1999
Aselin, Jeff 1994
Ask, Scott 1998
Austin, Manuel 1997-99

B

Bailey, Bruce 1991, 92
Bailey, Cary 1981
Bailey, Mario 1989-91
Bailey, Walter 1990, 91, 92
Baldassin, Mike 1974-76
Baldwin, Kenny 1983
Ballenger, Ken 1967-69
Barber, Rich 1984
Barnes, Bill 1964-66
Barry, Damon 1991, 92
Barry, Jay 1989-92
Battle, Eric 1994, 95
Baty, Rank 1969, 70
Bauer, Steve 1978

Bayard, Ralph 1969, 70
Bayle, David 1979, 80
Beall, Bruce 1985-87
Bean, Michael 1977
Beard, Colin 1998
Bearden, Garland 1984
Beaupain, Brooks 1994-96
Bell, Curtis 1987
Bell, Joe 1969, 70
Belmondo, Dave 1975
Benn, Kyle 1998, 99
Bennett, Steve 1997
Berg, Bob 1967-69
Bergman, Marv 1957
Bernhardi, Lee 1961, 62
Bertheau, Rene 1956, 57
Bethea, Cliff 1977
Beymer, Jim 1965
Bianchini, Paul 1974, 75
Bibbs, Dwight 1994
Binkley, Jesse 1995, 96
Bjornson, Eric 1991-94
Blanche, Sam 1999
Blacken, Ron 1978, 79, 80
Blanks, Harvey 1967, 68
Bledsoe, Mac 1965-67
Bond, Chuck 1963
Bonner, Glen 1972-73
Bonwell, Tony 1971, 72
Borders, Phil 1958
Boustead, Bob 1973, 74
Boyd, Skip 1972-74
Bracken, Joe 1986
Brady, John 1970-72
Bramwell, Steve 1963-65
Brandt, Gary 1964-66
Brandt, Rich 1957
Brennan, Bob 1981
Bresolin, Andy 1981
Breuner, Mark 1991-94
Bridge, Todd 1992
Brigham, Jeremy 1995-97
Briggs, Gary 1977-79
Briggs, Mike 1961-63

Brimhall, Dennis 1971
Briscoe, Eric 1987-90
Brock, Lee 1967-69
Bronson, Gordy 1975
Brooke, Deane 1975,76
Brooks, Greg 1975-77
Brose, Ted 1981
Brostek, Bern 1986-89
Brown, Bill 1985
Brown, Corey 1989
Brown, Dennis 1979-82
Brown, Dennis 1989-89
Brown, Reggie, 1973, 74
Browning, Charlie, 1962-64
Browning, Dave 1976, 77
Browning, Dean 1981, 82
Brownlee, Brandy 1987
Breuner, Mark 1991-94
Brunell, Mark 1990-92
Bryant, Beno 1989, 90, 91, 93
Buckland, Charlie 1971
Bulger, Ace 1968-70
Bullard, Barry 1958-60
Bullard, Tim 1960, 61
Burkhalter, Eugene 1987-89
Burleson, Al 1973-75
Burleson, Al Jr. 1997
Burnham, Tim 1984, 85
Burnham, Tom 1979, 80
Burmeister, Bob 1969, 70
Burrell, Eddie 1996
Burton, Nigel 1996-98
Bush, Blair 1975-77
Busz, Scott 1984-86
Butler, Hillary 1990-93
Butler, Toure 1997-2000
Bynum, Kai 1996

C

Cahill, Bill 1970-72
Caldwell, Tony 1980, 81
Call, Wes 1999, 2000
Camarillo, Rich 1979, 80
Campbell, Chris 1994-97
Canton, Eric 1988
Carnahan, Don 1962

Carr, Gary 1964, 65
Carr, Gary 1969, 70
Carr, Luther 1957, 58
Carroll, Andy 1997, 98, 99
Carrothers, Randy 1979
Carter, James 1980, 81
Casarino, Dario 1980
Cass, Greg 1965, 66
Cattage, Ray 1980, 81
Celoni, Dan 1973-75
Chambers, Richie 1991-94
Chandler, Chris 1984-87
Chandler, Jeff 1987-89
Chapman, John 1985
Chappell, Blaise 1983, 85
Chapple, Stan 1958-60
Chavira, Dan 1976-79
Chenevert, Cornelius 1974
Chicoine, Ryan 1997
Chorak, Jason 1994-97
Claridge, Bruce 1956-58
Claridge, Pat 1958-60
Clark, Gary 1961, 62
Clark, Ron 1965
Clawson, David 1979, 80,
Cleeland, Cameron 1994-97
Cleland, Thane 1983-86
Cleman, Braxton 1998, 99, 2000
Clifford, James 1988, 89, 91, 92
Coats, Tony 1995-98
Coby, Vince 1978, 81
Coffey, Junior 1962-64
Coker, Cliff 1966, 67
Cole, David 1986
Coleman, Fred 1994-97
Coleman, Randy 1970, 71
Collins, Brett 1988-91
Collins, Greg 1970-72
Collins, Michael 1981-83
Compton, James 1987 88, 89
Condon, Matt 1997, 98, 99
Conely, Ken 1973, 74
Conniff, Pat 1997-2000
Conklin, Cary 1988, 89
Connell, Kurth 1998, 99
Conrad, Pat 1981

Conwell, Ernie 1992-95
Cook, John 1989, 90
Cooney, Adam 1987-90
Cope, Jim 1966-68
Core, (Whitey) John 1955-57
Cornell, Bo 1968-70
Coty, Paul 1980, 81, 82
Covington, Tony 1985-88
Cowan, Tim 1980, 81, 82
Coyle, Michael 1997
Crabbe, Jason 1991, 93
Craig, Al 1969, 70, 71
Crawford, Mike 1957, 59
Cromer, Marshall 1976-78
Crow, Doug 1982, 83, 84
Cuesta, Tony 1976
Cunningham, Dan 1969, 70
Cunningham, Ed 1989-91
Cunningham, Francois 1982
Cupic, Steve 1977
Curtis, Mike 1977, 1980

D

Dahlquist, Eric 1984
Dalan, Aaron 1995-98
Daley, Bill 1982
Daniels, Darrell 1997-2000
Darden, Michael 1988
Dasso, Gary 1959
Daste, Dominic 1996, 98-2000
Davidson, Ben 1959, 60
Davillier, Craig 1975
Davis, James 1979
Davis, Reggie 1995-98
Davis, Wondame 1998, 99,
Dawson, Dave 1996-2000
Day, Dick 1955-57
Day, Mark 1969, 71
Dean, Fred 1974
DeFeo, Brenno 1981, 83, 84
DeGross, Mark 1987-90
Derrow, Mike 1991
DeSausssure, Andre 1995, 98
Devers, Deke 1993, 94, 95
Dibble, Robb 1994
Dicks, Norm 1961, 62

Diehl, Bill 1963
Dillon, Dave 1965, 66
Dillon, Corey 1996
Dinish, Dave 1965
Dinish, Dom 1969
Dochow, Mike 1973
Doctor, William 1988-91
Dodd, Mike 1990
Dodson, Lance 1981, 82, 83
Doheny, Brian 1971-73
Dominque, Tony 1983, 85
Douglas, Bill 1962-64
Dow, Don 1979, 80, 81
Downey, Darrell 1970, 72
Doyle, Pat 1987, 88
Driscoll, Ken 1979, 80, 81
Dumas, Larry 1971
Dunn, Bob 1957
Dunn, Dick 1960
Dunn, Roger 1964, 65
DuPree, Dave 1966, 67
Dykes, Trent 1998

E

Earl, Randy 1975
Earl, Robin 1976
Easton, Roy 1969, 70
Echols, Bob 1957-59
Edwards, John 1975-77
Edwards, Renard 1998, 99
Eernissee, Dan 1982-84
Eicher, Jim 1971
Elstrom, Todd 1998-2000
Elswick, Pete 1971-73
Emerson, P.A. 1990, 93
Emtman, Steve 1989-91
Enders, Dave 1970-72
Enslow, Dave 1957, 60
Erlandson, Tom 1985-87
Esary, Tim 1987
Everett, Jim 1961
Ewaliko, Mike 1993-95

F

Failla, Tom 1968-70
Farr, D'Marco 1991-93

Fauria, Lance 1984
Fausett, Scott 1980, 81
Feigner, Nick 1999
Feleay, Don 1975, 76
Fenney, Rick 1983-86
Ferguson, Al 1957
Ferguson, Bob 1970-72
Fiala, John 1993-96
Fields, Jaime 1989-92
Fink, Rob 1969
Fitzgerald, Scott 1987, 88
Fitzpatrick, Denny 1973, 74
Flemming, George 1958-60
Flemming, Ryan 1998, 99
Flewelling, Roger 1967
Flick, Tom 1979, 80
Folkins, Lee 1958-60
Foreman, Phil 1976, 77, 79
Forsberg, Fred 1963-65
Fortney, Shane 1994-96
Fountaine, Jamal 1990-93
Fraize, Matt 1997-99
Fraley, Chico 1988-91
Franklin, Darryl 1984-87
Fudzie, Vince 1985
Fuller, Brian 1999
Fuimano, Andy 1982, 85

G

Gaffney, Mike 1984-86
Gagliardi, Bret 1976-80
Gains, Robert 1975-77
Gains, Spider 1978
Gallagher, Tom 1991-93
Galoia, Willy 1975-78
Galuska, Dick 1969-71
Garcia, Frank 1991-94
Gardenhire, John 1980, 81
Gardner, Ken 1978, 79, 80
Garland, John 1969
Garnett, Scott 1980, 81
Garrett, Leon 1975, 76
Gayton, Carver 1957-59
Gegner, Kurt 1958-60
Gehring, Rob 1974-76
Gaspard, Curtis 1990, 91

George, Odell 1998
Gipson, Ron 1975-79
Glasgow, Nesby 1975-78
Glennon Bill, 1965-67
Gogan, Kevin 1984-86
Gorman, Don 1971, 72
Gosselin, Dan 1969, 1971
Goudeau, Marc 1988
Grant, Ron 1977
Graves, Bob 1973, 74
Green, Mike 1973-75
Green, Phil 1992
Green, Roderick 1999
Greene, Danny 1980, 81, 83, 84
Greenwood, Scott 1976-78
Greenlee, Tom 1964-66
Greenwood, Scott 1975-77
Gregory, Rusty 1974, 75
Griffith, Clay 1986
Grimes, Greg 1977, 78, 79
Guinn, Gordy 1970-72

H

Habib, Brian 1986, 87
Hadley, Ron 1983-85
Hagen, Koll 1962-64
Halverson, Dean 1965-67
Hamer, Ken 1980
Hanzlik, Steve 1969
Hairston, Marques 1995-99
Hairston, Russell 1992-94
Hall, Dana 1988-91
Hall, Darryl 1986-88
Hammon, Ira 1970
Hannah, Mark 1968, 69
Hanson, Travis 1990-92
Harrell, Bruce 1976-79
Harris, Eugene 1992
Harris, Gerald 1996-2000
Harris, Jason 1996-98
Harris, Jim 1967-69
Harrison, Martin 1986-89
Harvey, Chet 1957
Harvey Derek 1979, 80, 81
Hart, John 1999
Hasselbach, Harold 1989

Hatem, Ossim 1999
Hawkins, Dejuan 1999
Hawkins, Pedro 1975-77
Hayes, Andre 1995
Hayes, Rick 1970, 71, 73
Haynes, Lenny 1998, 99
Heck, Jim 1956-58
Heinrich, Kyle 1976-78
Heinz, Robbie 1962-64
Hemphill, Frank 1975
Hendricks, Willie 1973, 74
Hewitt, Lynn 1961, 62
Hicks, Antony 1996, 97
Hicks, Matt 1995
Hicks, Richard 1989, 90
Highfield, Trevor 1993, 94, 95
Hill, Lonzel 1983-86
Hill, Stewart 1981-83
Hinds, Sterling 1981-83
Hinds, Steve 1963-65
Hivner, Bob 1958-60
Hobart, Billy Joe 1991
Hoffman, Chris 1996
Hoffman, Dave 1989-92
Hoffman, Steve 1992, 94, 95
Holliman, Terry 1994, 95
Hollowell, Alex 1996
Holmes, Ron 1982-84
Holzgraf, Steve 1985, 86
Hooker, Ja'Warren 1997, 98
Hooks, Wilbur 1999
Hopkins, Hoover 1983
Horton, Ray 1979-82
Houlihan, Barry 1972
Houston, Herman 1969
Huard, Brock 1996-98
Huard, Damon 1993-95
Hudson, Ron 1966, 67
Huget, Jeff 1966-68
Huget, Rick 1969-71
Hullin, Todd 1964, 65
Hunt, Walt 1983, 84
Hunter, Art 1987-89
Hurley, Dennis 1968, 70
Hurst, Willie 1998, 99, 2000
Hurworth, Sam 1958-60

Hutt, Brad 1997, 98
Hyatt, Gary 1986

I

Ingalls, Jerry 1971

J

Jackson, Charles 1975
Jackson, Mike 1975-78
Jackson, Ray 1959, 60
Jackson, Ray 1980, 81,
Jackson, Ron 1980-84
Jackson, Vestee 1983-85
Jakl, Larry 1966
James, Allen 1983-86
James, Chris 1980, 81
James, Gary 1967, 68
Janet, Ernie 1968-70
Janoski, Dave 1993-96
Janowicz, Vince 1966, 67
Jarvis, Bruce 1968-70
Jarzynka, Joe 1996-99
Jenkins, Aaron 1985-88
Jenkins, Fletcher 1979, 80, 81
Jenson, Jason 1990
Jenson, Jerry 1994-97
Jerome, Todd 1989
Jerue, Mark 1979-81
Johanson, Bob 1976
John-Lewis, Kelly 1987, 88
Johnson, Clifton 1979
Johnson, Devon 1999
Johnson, Jeff 1997, 98
Johnson, Leif 1990-93
Johnson, Lynn 1994, 96
Johnson, Todd 1996-98
Johnson, Tom 1986
Jolley, Chris 1989
Jones, Brendan 1996, 98
Jones, Calvin 1970, 71, 72
Jones, Darius 1995
Jones, Donald 1988-91
Jones, Frank 1976
Jones, Jim 1955-57
Jones, Joe 1959, 60
Jones, Louis 1991-94

Jones, Marc 1989
Jones, Matt 1990-93
Jones, Rod 1984-86
Jones, Scott 1985-88
Jones, Steve 1986-88
Jones, Virgil 1988, 90
Jordan, Jeff 1964-66
Jorgensen, Kermit 1959-61
Jourdan, Roberto 1972-74
Juergens, Chris 1998, 99
Jugum, George 1966-68
Julian, Ryan 1998, 2000

K

Kadletz, Ben 1996-98
Kadletz, Jon 1969
Kadletz, Ryan 1994, 95
Kahn, Dan 1987
Kaligis, Pete 1991
Kaloper, Jerry 1968
Kasim, Marvin 1998
Katsenes, Jim 1970
Kaufman, Napoleon 1991-94
Keely, Rick 1969
Keiaho, George 1995, 96
Kelly, Anthony 1999, 2000
Kelly, Joe 1992-95
Kelso, Al 1971, 72
Kennen, Washington 1971-73
Kennamer, Buddy 1968, 69
Kennedy, Lincoln 1989-92
Kerley, Doug 1977,78
Kerley, John 1976-78
Kesi, Patrick 1992-95
Kesi, Petrocelli 1996, 97
Kester, Todd 1987
Keyes, Stewart 1983
Kezer, Glen 1961, 62
Killpatrick, David 1991-94
Kilpack, Mark 1987, 88
Kinnune, Bill 1958-69
Kirk, Jim 1965, 66
Kirkland, Dean 1988-90
Kirkpatrick, James 1982-84
Kissel, Cam 1994-96
Knoll, Jerry 1962-64

Knoll, Jon 1962-64
Knopp, Brett 1999
Kohlwes, Jeff 1987, 88
Kopay, Dave 1961, 62
Kopay, Tony 1961
Krakoski, Joe 1981-84
Kralik, Joe 1990-93
Krammer, Bruce 1964, 65
Kravitz, Al 1970, 71
Kreutz, Mark 1973, 74
Kreutz, Olin 1995-97
Krieg, Jim 1970, 71
Kristof, Jim 1972-74
Kroon, Bruce 1984
Kuharski, Rob 1982, 83
Kupp, Jake 1961-63

L

Labrousse, Dave 1975
Lacson, Alex 1995
Lal, Sunjay 1991
Lambright, Eric 1984, 85
Lambright, Jim 1963, 64
Lang, Chris 1995, 98
Lang, Le-Lo 1986-89
Lansford, Mike 1978, 79
Larson, Mark 1984-86
Larson, Tom 1999
Leaphart, Robert 1981
Lee, Ken 1967, 68, 70
Lee, Kyu 1999
Lee, Mark 1976-79
Leeland, Jeff 1976-78
Leland, Dave 1957
Lentz, Nick 1997
Lewis, Greg 1988-90
Lewis, Tony 1983, 84
Libke, Al 1963-65
Lightening, Shawn 1987
Lindquist, Reese 1956-58
Linnin, Chris 1978, 79
Lipe, Steve 1973-1975
Lloyd, Dan 1972-74
Locknane, Brent 1987
Locknane, Duane 1960-62
Loomis, Scott 1971, 72

Long, Scott 1976, 77
Looker, Dane 1998, 99
Lorrain, Vince 1965, 66
Lovelien, Bob 1968-70
Lowe, Omare 1998, 99, 2000
Lowell, Duane 1956-58
Lutes, Dave 1974, 75
Lutu, Leroy 1980, 81
Lustyk, Mike 1989, 90, 92
Lutu, Frank 1986, 87
Lutu, Leroy 1980, 82, 83
Lyons, Lamar 1991-94

M

Mack, Damon 1991, 92
Mackie, Brent 1978
Mackey, Willie Ray 1979
Madarieta, Levi 1999
Madsen, Lynn 1981-83
Maggart, Mike 1966-68
Mahdavi, Ben 1999, 2000
Maher, Dennis 1981-84
Malamala, Siupeli 1988-91
Malloe, Ikaika 1993-96
Mallory, Rick 1981-83
Malone, Art 1985-88
Malvar, Caesar 1989
Mancuso, Joe 1963, 65
Manke, Tom 1967, 68
Manfield, Ray 1960-62
Marcinowski, Adam 1999
Marcus, Clifton 1973, 74
Marona, Spencer 1999, 2000
Marquiss, Guy 1975
Marsh, Curt 1976-80
Marshall, Bill 1981
Martin, Bob 1971, 74
Martin, Don 1965-67
Martin, Doug 1976-79
Martin, Greg 1975
Mason, Andy 1990-93
Mathews, Jim 1985
Matthews, David 1981
Matthews, Keilan 1985, 86
Matter, Kurt 1970
Matthews, David 1981

Matz, Mike 1985-89
Mauer, Al 1969, 70
Mays, Shell 1991
Mays, Stafford 1978, 79
McBride, Cliff 1976
McCabe, Jim 1966, 67
McCallum, John 1988, 89
McCarter, Jim 1957
McCarthy, D.J. 1993
McClain, Jerry 1978, 79, 80
McClinton, Dave 1968
McCluskey, Mike 1956-58
McCumby, Don 1955-57
McDonald, Mark 1973, 74
McFarland, Murphy 1972, 73
McHale, Rick 1965-67
McKasson, Roy 1958-60
McKay, Orlando 1989-91
McKeta, Don 1958-60
McLain, Curt 1977
McLeod, Rick 1986, 87
McMahon Mark 1969,70
Mcnair, Troy 1989
McVeigh, Dick, 1957
Meamber, Tim 1981-84
Medved, Ron 1963-65
Meyer, Ricky 1985-87
Meyers, John 1959-61
Michael, Larry 1982, 83
Middleton, Bob 1969
Miletich, Ryan 1998, 99,
Millen, Hugh 1984, 85
Miller, Fred 1970-72
Miller, Mel 1996, 97
Millich, Don 1957, 59
Mills, Lamar 1968
Milloy, Lawyer 1993-95
Milus, Ron 1982-85
Mincy, Charles 1989, 90
Mitchell, Charlie 1960-62
Mitchell, James 1986
Mitchell, Lamar 1990
Mitchell, Mason 1964
Mizen, Anthony 1996-99
Monroe, Bob 1960-62
Moon, Warren 1977, 78

Moore, Don 1965, 66
Moore, Josh , 1991, 92
Moore, Shaun 1992
Mora, Jim 1981-83
Moraga, Rudy 1976-79
Morehead, Donnie 1984
Morgan, Carl 1957
Morgan, Quentin 1999
Moran, Eric 1980-82
Morrison, Steve 1995
Moses, Wayne 1973, 74, 76, 77,
Mulitauaopele, Toalei 1998, 99

N

Nakane, Tom 1992
Navarro, Joel 1986
Nelson, Chuck 1980-82
Nelson, John 1961
Nelson, Tom 1969
Nelson, Roger 1998, 99, 2000
Nettles, Aaron 1995
Neubauer, Lance 1979, 80
Nevelle, Jim 1991-93
Newsome, Vince 1979, 80, 81
Nicholl, Dick 1958
Ninanabu, Justin 1997
Norton, Jim 1962-64
Norwood, Lyle 1964, 65
Noeltner, Rick 1976
Nykreim , Mike 1975

O

O'Bannon, Mike 1964
O'Brien, John 1963
O'Connor, Chris 1979, 80, 81
O'Laughlin, Sean 1997, 98
Ohler, Pete 1961, 62
Oldes, Walter 1972, 73
Olson, Benji 1995-97
Olson. Ron 1975
Olson, Rusty 1979, 80
Olson, Vern 1976
Olszewski, Nick 1999, 2000
Otis, Mike 1963-65

P

Pahukoa, Jeff 1987, 89, 90
Pahukoa, Shane 1989-92
Pallis, Chris 1980
Papagergiou, George 1978
Parker, Bill 1966
Parker, Omar 1964-66
Parks, Ralph 1981
Parrish, Tony 1994-97
Parry, Doug 1987
Partridge, Jeff 1981, 82
Pathon, Jerome 1995-97
Pattison, Mark 1982-84
Paysano, Dick 1955-57
Pear, Dave 1972-74
Peasely, Ed 1957-59
Pearson, J.C. 1983, 84
Pederson, Bob 1965-67
Pederson, Mike 1979
Pelluer, Steve 1981
Pence, Jim 1977, 78, 79
Peoples, Tim 1982-86
Petermann, Nelse 1973, 74
Peters, Rashad 1999
Peterson, Andrew 1991-94
Petrich, Doug 1987
Pettigrew, Jim 1973
Pharms, Jeremiah 1997-2000
Phillips, Dave 1960-62
Phillips, Scott 1973-76
Pierce, Aaron 1988-91
Pierson, Pete 1991-93
Piety, John 1962
Pinney, Ray 1973, 74
Pitt, George 1957-59
Pittman, Bryan 1997
Plumley, Dave 1967
Poole, Mark 1987, 88
Pope, Steve 1978, 80
Porras, Tom 1978, 79,
Posey, Dan 1991
Preston, Ron 1969, 70
Price, Gary 1962
Prince, Geoff 1994-96

Q

Quesada, Greg 1994-95
Quinn, Lou 1973-75

R

Rainwater, Dwayne 1992
Randle, Ivory 1988
Ray, Eddie 1974, 75
Reddick, Patrick 1997
Reed, Frank 1975
Reed, Mike 1994, 96, 97
Reed, William, 1980
Redman, Rick 1962-64
Reilly, Mike 1979, 80
Richardson, Antowine 1976-79
Richardson, Bob 1965-67
Richardson, Keith 1977, 78, 79
Richardson, Kevin 1975,76
Richardson, Travis 1987-90
Richie, David 1993-95
Rideout, Will 1986, 87
Riley, Andre 1986-89
Rill, David 1984-87
Rios, Augie 1967-69
Robbins, Mitch 1987
Robbins, Steve 1975-77
Roberson, Dan 1969
Roberts, Jay 1984-87
Roberts, Kyle 1996, 97
Roberts, Steve 1985, 86
Robertson, Al 1983, 84
Robinson, Dante 1991, 92
Robinson, Jacque 1981-84
Roche, Wayne 1976-78
Rodwell, Dain 1971
Roehl, Tom 1971, 72
Rodgers, Jim 1980, 81, 83, 84
Rodgers, Tyrone 1990, 91
Rogers, Reggie 1984-86
Rohrbach, Mike 1975-77
Rongen, Kris 1991
Ronnebaum, Lane 1968-70
Rosborough, Willie 1980-82
Rose, Carl 1973
Rowland, Chris 1973-75
Rowland, Ron 1976, 77,
Rumberger, Trip 1977

Ryan, Joe 1962, 63
Ryan, Mike 1964-66

S

Safford, Don 1962, 63
Sampson, Jim 1963, 64
Sanders, Eugene 1974
Sanford, Joe 1976, 78, 79
Sanford, Steve 1966
Sapp, Bob 1994-96
Sarieddine, Sacha 1999
Sarshar, Hamid 1996
Sartoris, Jim 1964, 66
Saunders, Calvin 1978
Savini, Sauni 1984
Sawyer, James 1988
Scheyer, Paul 1964
Scheyer, Rod 1960-62
Schlamp, Dean 1975
Schlepp, Eric 1995
Schloredt, Bob 1958-60
Schmidt, Donovan 1991-94
Schmit, Joel 1979
Schoepper, Bob 1967, 68
Schulberg, Rick 1989, 90
Schulte, Steve 1970-72
Schwartz, Avery 1966, 68
Scott, J.K, 1999, 2000
Scott, Tom 1971, 72
Seida, Judd 1998
Seminavage, Opu 1995
Sharp, Rick 1967-69
Shavey, Gary 1996, 97
Shaw, Maurice 1996, 97, 99
Sheperd, Ron 1970, 72
Shehee, Rashaan 1994-97
Shelley, Jason 1992
Shelton, Geoff 1999
Sherwood, Terry 1976, 77, 79
Shoe, Jeff 1995
Siler, Bill 1961, 62
Silvers, Elliot 1998, 99, 2000
Simpson, Jim 1986
Sixkiller, Sonny 1970-72
Skaggs, Jim 1959-61
Skansi, John 1983

Skansi, Phil 1979-82
Skurski, Jim 1998, 99
Slater, Brian 1985-88
Sligh, Luther 1969, 71, 72
Simmons, Joe 1975
Small, Fred 1981-84
Smith, Bob 1977
Smith, Brett 1984, 85
Smith, Chris 1979
Smith, Danianke 1990, 91
Smith, David 1981
Smith, Frank 1966, 67
Smith, Greg 1974
Smith, George 1986, 88
Smith, Jermaine 1996-99
Smith, Josh 1995-98
Smith, Rob 1975, 76, 78
Smith, Shannon 1983
Smith, Tommie 1989-92
Smith, Tommie 1989
Snider, Bill 1957
Sobbi, Mostafa 1995, 96
Soldat, Dennis 1983-85
Sortun, Rick 1961-63
Sparlin, Tom 1966, 67
Spearman, Tony 1982
Spiesterbach, Don 1966-68
Springstead, Steve 1990-93
Sprinkle, Bill 1967, 68
Stanley, Rod 1971, 73
Stapleton, Bill 1979, 80, 81
Steele, Chuck 1961
Steele, Joe 1976-79
Stephans, Dale 1964, 65
Stevens, Jerramy 1999
Stevens, Kyle 1977-80
Stewart, Mark 1979-82
Stifter, Bill 1965
Stiger, Jim 1961, 62
Stone, Brian 1980, 81
Stransky, Dave 1982, 83
Strohmeier, Paul 1975
Stromswold, Dave 1975, 76
Stroud, Mike 1964
Stuart, Scott 1991
Stupey, John 1961-63

Sublet, Tam 1987
Summers, Matt 1997
Sweatt, Dick 1970, 71
Sweet, Carl 1969

T

Tabor, Joe 1972, 73
Taggares, Pete 1971-73
Tamble, Geoff 1994
Tarver, Roger 1980, 81, 83
Tharps, Terry 1999
Theoudele, Lance 1976-79
Thomas, Garth 1984-86
Thomas, Justin 1992-94
Thomas, Richard 1992-95
Thompson, Scott 1980, 82
Thompson, Steve 1965-67
Toews, Jeff 1975-78
Tormey, Pete 1977, 78, 79
Towns, Lester 1996-99
Toy, David 1984-87
Travis, greg 1986-89
Trimble, David 1981, 83, 84, 85
Tripplett, Larry 1999
Tufono, Albert 1983, 84, 87
Tuiaea, Mac 1996-99
Tuiasosopo, Marques 1997-2000
Turner, Darius 1989-92
Turner, Mark 1968, 70
Turnure, Tom 1977, 78, 79,
Tlyer, Toussaint 1977-80
Tymer, Tom 1971

V

Van Divier, Randy 1980
Van Hoosier, Paul 1981
Van Valkenberg, Carl 1975, 76
Verti, Tom 1967-69
Vicino, Mike 1975
Volbrecht, Ron 1968-70
Vonture, Anthony 1999, 2000

W

Waddell, Chris 1999
Wagner, Paul 1982
Walderhaug, Stan 1975-77

Wales, John 1994-96
Walker, Dave 1985
Walker, Ken 1998
Walker, Lacey 1983
Wallin, Steve 1971, 72
Wallrof, Paul 1957
Walters, Jack 1957-59
Ward, Chad 1997-2000
Wardlow, Don 1975-77
Ware, Keven 1999
Washington, Dee 1974
Washington, Otis 1967, 68
Waskom, Bob 1985
Waskom, Jim 1987, 88
Waskom, Paul 1984-86
Waters, Bert 1955
Waters, Donalt T. 1973
Watts, Jerry 1971
Wea, Gerald 1966, 67
Weathersby, Vince 1985-88
Weatherspoon, Hakim 1998
Weindl, Jamie 1993
Wenger, Barry 1968
Werdel, John 1991-93
Werner, Clyde 1967-69
Wesley, Don 1972
West, Marc 1989
Westlund, Roger 1975-78
Weston, Doug 1979, 81, 82
Westra, John 1997, 98
Wetterauer, Dick 1963-65
Weyrick, Alan 1989
Wheeler, Ron 1979, 80
Whitacre, John 1972,73
White, Bob 1957-59
White, Cedric 1993
Whitenight, David, 1981
Whitmyer, Nat 1961, 62
Wiese, Brett 1985-88
Wiezbowski, Steve 1970-72
Wiggs, Sekou 1995-97
Williams, Aaron 1979-81
Williams, Curtis 1998, 99, 2000
Williams, Dave 1964-66
Williams, Demouy 1985-87
Williams, Greg 1979, 80

Williams, Jafar, 1998, 99, 2000
Williams, Jerry 1964-66
Willig, Bob 1985-88
Willis, Dave 1986
Willis, Don 1993
Willis, Gene 1968, 69, 71
Willis, Jamaun 1999
Wilmoth, Jeff 1984
Wilson, Aaron 1977, 78
Wilson, Darren 1983
Wilson, Kirk 1957, 58
Wilson, Stan 1975, 76
Winters, Ralph 1963-65
Witcher, Darren 1980-82
Wojcjechowski, Carl 1967, 68
Wold, Ron 1978
Woldseth, Hans 1972, 73
Wolfe, Chad 1995
Wood, Harrison 1966-68
Wooten, Brent 1958-60
Wroten, Tony 1981-84
Worgan, Dave 1970-72
Worley, Al 1966-68
Worley, Larry 1970
Wrotten, Tony 1981
Wyatt, Martin 1961, 62
Wyles, Channing 1989, 90

Y

Yates, Bo 1984-87

Z

Zachery, Tony 1985-88
Zajac, Elliot 1999, 2000
Zakskorn, Pat 1980, 81, 82
Zandofsky, Mike 1985-88
Zatkovich, Dick 1967
Zeger, John 1980, 81

1957

Record: 3-6-1   **Finish:** PCC 6th   **Coach:** Jim Owens

Date	UW	Opponent		Attendance
Sept. 21	6	Colorado	6	34,684
Sept. 28	7	at Minnesota	46	63,512
Oct. 5	7	Ohio State	35	36,328
Oct. 12	0	at UCLA	19	24,889
Oct. 19	14	Stanford	21	36,036
Oct. 26	19	Oregon State	6	29,231
Nov. 2	12	Southern Cal	19	30,172
Nov. 9	13	Oregon (Portland)	6	30,010
Nov. 16	35	at California	27	38,000
Nov. 23	7	Wash. State	27	47,352
Totals:	120		212	370,214

Co-Captains: Whitey Core, Jim Jones

Honors

Guy Flaherty: Dick Payseno. **L. Walt Rising:** Whitey Core. **All-Coast:** Marv Bergman, Jim Jones.

Commentary

The Jim Owens era began with a 6-6 tie against Colorado. At mid-season the Huskies were 0-4-1 and facing Oregon State, the defending Pacific Coast Champions, who had played in the 1957 Rose Bowl against Iowa. The Huskies were heavy underdogs, but stunned Oregon State 19-6. The first win of the year seemed to jump start the team and another upset followed over Oregon, 13-6, in Portland. California was the next Husky victim, 35-27, the first victory by a Washington team in Berkeley in 13 years. What remains the hallmark of the 1957 team is what *Seattle Post-Intelligencer* sports writer, Mike Donohoe, called the *death march*. No one is certain what effect it actually had on the success or lack of success of the 1957 squad. What it did do without question was give birth to the Husky mystique of a Marine attitude about discipline and work ethic.

Lettermen

Don Armstrong	Dave Enslow	Dick McVeigh
Marv Bergmann	Al Ferguson	Don Millich
Rene Bertheau	Chet Harvey	Carl Morgan
Rich Brandt	Jim Heck	Dick Payseno
Luther Carr	Jim Jones	Ed Peasely
Bruce Claridge	Dave Leland	George Pitt
Whitey Core	Reese Lindquist	Bill Snider
Mike Crawford	Duane Lowell	Paul Wallrof
Dick Day	Jim McCarter	Jack Walters
Bob Dunn	Mike McCluskey	Bob White
Bob Echols	Don McCumby	Kirk Wilson

1958

Record: 3-7-0		Finish: PCC - 8th		Coach: Jim Owens
Date	**UW**	**Opponent**		**Attendance**
Sept. 20	14	San Jose State	6	29,395
Sept. 27	24	Minnesota	21	38,716
Oct. 4	7	at Ohio State	12	79,477
Oct. 11	12	at Stanford	22	26,384
Oct. 18	0	UCLA	20	34,594
Oct. 25	12	Oregon St.(Portland)	14	29,514
Nov. 1	6	Oregon	0	33,225
Nov. 8	6	at Southern Cal	21	33,083
Nov. 15	7	California	12	30,980
Nov. 22	14	Wash. State (Spokane)	18	24,051
Totals:	**102**		**146**	**359,419**

Captains: game co-captains

Honors

Guy Flaherty: Don Armstrong. **L. Walt Rising:** Don Armstrong

Commentary

This remains the youngest ever Husky team: 10 sophomores were in the starting lineup against San Jose State on opening day at Husky Stadium. While the season won-lose record actually declined to 3-7 it was deceiving. As example the rematch with Minnesota was the season highlight as the Huskies avenged a 46-7 blowout in 1957 to upset the Gophers in Seattle 24-21. That was followed with a trip to Columbus, Ohio for a re-match with Big Ten champion Ohio State. It was expected to be an easy victory for Rose Bowl champion Ohio State under coach Woody Hayes, but it was anything but easy as the 12-7 final score reflected. The Huskies scored only one other victory in 1958, once again upsetting Oregon, who had played in the Rose Bowl against Ohio State. But the season ending loss to Washington State in Spokane, 18-14, revealed that this young team had taken to heart the Jim Owens' brand of football.

Lettermen

Chuck Allen	Lee Folkins	Roy McKasson
Don Armstrong	Carver Gayton	Don McKeta
Phil Borders	Kurt Gegner	Dick Nicholl
Barry Bullard	Jim Heck	Ed Peasely
Luther Carr	Bob Hivner	George Pitt
Stan Chapple	Sam Hurworth	Bob Schloredt
Bruce Claridge	Bill Kinnune	Jack Walters
Pat Claridge	Reese Lindquist	Bob White
Bob Echols	Duane Lowell	Kirk Wilson
George Flemming	Mike McCloskey	Brent Wooten

1959

Record 10-1-0		Finish: AAWU lst		Coach: **Jim Owens**
Date	**UW**	**Opponent**		**Attendance**
Sept. 19	21	at Colorado	12	27,000
Sept. 25	23	Idaho	0	24,476
Oct. 3	51	Utah	6	27,560
Oct. 10	10	Stanford	0	36,713
Oct. 17	15	Southern Cal	22	54,497
Oct. 24	13	Oregon (Portland)	12	37,000
Oct. 31	23	at UCLA	7	32,878
Nov. 7	13	Oregon State	6	45,317
Nov. 14	20	at California	0	38,800
Nov. 21	20	Washington State	0	55,782
Jan. 1	44	Wisconsin (Rose Bowl)	8	100,809
Totals:	**253**		**73**	**480,792**

Captains: game co-captains

Honors

Guy Flaherty: Don McKeta. **L. Walt Rising:** Kurt Gegner. **Brian Stapp:** Dick Dunn.
All-American: Bob Schloredt. **All-Coast:** Chuck Allen, Kurt Gegner, Bob Schloredt.
AP & UPI West Coast Player of the Year: Bob Schloredt.

Commentary

No one was ready for this Husky team. Certainly not Husky fans: in the previous 17 seasons the Husky record was 68 wins, 82 loses, and 7 ties. The last Husky Rose Bowl team was 1936. During the regular season the Husky defense surrendered only 65 points and recorded four shutouts. No other Husky defense since has come close to that record, not even the unbeaten Husky national championship team of 1991. Finally the Rose Bowl game against Wisconsin's Badgers. Because Big Ten teams had dominated the Rose Bowl series agaist the West Coast teams by winning 11 of the previous 12 games, experts favored Wisconsin by 10 to 14 points. The stunning 44-8 Washington victory brought about a new era of Husky football and a renaissance to West Coast football that continues until today. This team is still the measuring stick when it comes to playing with heart and spirit.

Lettermen

Chuck Allen	Carver Gayton	Don Millich
Dick Aguirre	Kurt Gegner	Ed Peasely
Barry Bullard	Bob Hivner	George Pitt
Stan Chapple	Sam Hurworth	Bob Schloredt
Pat Claridge	Ray Jackson	Jim Skaggs
Mike Crawford	Joe Jones	Jack Walters
Gary Dasso	Kermit Jorgensen	Dan Wheatley
Ben Davidson	Bill Kinnune	Bob White
Bob Echols	Roy McKasson	Brent Wooten
George Flemming	Don McKeta	
Lee Folkins	John Meyers	

1960

Record: 10-1-0		Finish: AAWU - lst		Coach: Jim Owens
Date	**UW**	**Opponent**		**Attendance**
Sept. 17	55	Pacific	6	39,047
Sept. 24	41	Idaho	12	35,996
Oct. 1	14	Navy	15	57,379
Oct. 8	29	at Stanford	10	24,032
Oct. 15	10	UCLA	8	54,152
Oct. 22	30	Oregon St.(Portland)	29	36,823
Oct. 29	7	Oregon	6	55,235
Nov. 5	34	Southern Cal	0	43,475
Nov. 12	27	California	7	55,884
Nov. 19	8	Wash. St. (Spokane)	7	28,750
Total	**272**		**107**	**528,097**

Co-Captains: Game Co-Captains

Honors

Guy Flaherty: Don McKeta. **L. Walt Rising:** Roy McKasson. **Brian Stapp:** Jim Everett.

All-America: Roy McKasson. **All-Coast**: Roy McKasson, Kurt Gegner, Chuck Allen, Don McKeta, George Flemming, Ray Jackson.

Commentary

With every starter returning from the Rose Bowl every team on their schedule had a bull's eye on the date when they played the Huskies. But the Huskies only stumbled once, against Navy, a 15-14 loss at home when Greg Mather kicked a field goal with 14 seconds left in the game. A final irony was that the team that prided itself on always winning the fourth quarter suffered their only two loses in two years in the fourth quarter! In the Rose Bowl Minnesota was the Big Ten opponent and once again the Huskies were considered underdogs by the experts. The Huskies had to prove themselves one more time and they did beating Minnesota 17-7. Bob Schloredt once again was voted the games Most Valuable Player.

Lettermen

Dick Aguirre	Lee Folkins	Don McKeta
Andy Alkire	Kurt Gegner	Charlie Mitchell
Chuck Allen	Bob Hivner	Bob Monroe
Barry Bullard	Sam Hurworth	John Meyers
Tim Bullard	Ray Jackson	Dave Phillips
Stan Chapple	Bill Kinnune	Rod Scheyer
Pat Claridge	Duane Locknane	Bob Schloredt
Ben Davidson	Joe Jones	Jim Skaggs
Dick Dunn	Kermit Jorgensen	Brent Wooten
Dave Enslow	Ray Mansfield	
George Flemming	Roy McKasson	

1961

Record 5-4-1		**Finish**: AAWU tie 2nd		**Coach**: Jim Owens
Date	**UW**	**Opponent**		**Attendance**
Sept. 23	6	Purdue	13	54,752
Sept. 30	20	at Illinois	7	41,319
Oct. 7	22	Pittsburgh	17	54,411
Oct. 14	14	at California	21	43,000
Oct. 21	13	Stanford	0	52,741
Oct. 28	6	Oregon (Portland)	7	32,681
Nov. 4	0	Southern Cal	0	54,916
Nov. 11	0	Oregon State	3	49,652
Nov. 18	17	at UCLA	13	33,969
Nov. 21	21	Washington State	17	49,676
Totals	**119**		98	467,117

Co-Captains: John Meyers, Kermit Jorgensen.

Honors

Guy Flaherty: John Meyers. **L. Walt Rising:** John Meyers. **Brian Stapp:** Jim Everett. **All-Coast:** John Meyers, Jim Skaggs, Charlie Mitchell.

Commentary

With every starter graduated from the 1960 and 1961 Rose Bowl teams, except tackle John Meyers, this was expected to be a rebuilding season for the Huskies. Yet except for one or two plays the Huskies could have returned to the Rose Bowl for a third straight year. The problem wasn't defense; the Huskies gave up a total of only 98 points for the entire season, but could score only 119 points on offense. The plays which sunk their Rose Bowl hopes were a blocked punt in the Cal game at Berkeley which resulted in a 21-14 lose, a failed 4th and inches run at the Oregon goal line by Kermit Jorgensen in a 7-6 loss, and a 50- yard touchdown run by Jorgensen in the Southern Cal game which was called back because of a penalty that resulted in a 0-0 tie. Three plays resulted in two loses and a tie. If the 1959 and 1960 teams could be called a *team called desire* the 1961 Husky team could have been called *a farewell to arms* for its lack of offense.

Lettermen

Andy Alkire	Tony Kopay	Dave Phillips
Lee Bernhardi	Glen Kezer	Rod Schuyer
Mike Briggs	Jake Kupp	Bill Siler
Tim Bullard	Duane Locknane	Jim Skaggs
Gary Clark	Ray Mansfield	Rick Sortun
Norm Dicks	John Meyers	Chuck Steel
Jim Everett	Charlie Mitchell	Jim Stiger
Lynn Hewitt	Bob Monroe	John Stupey
Kermit Jorgensen	John Nelson	Nate Whitmyer
Dave Kopay	Pete Ohler	Martin Wyatt

1962

Record: 7-2-1		Finish: AAWU 2nd		Coach: Jim Owens
Date	UW	Opponent		Attendance
Sept. 22	7	Purdue	7	56,076
Sept. 29	28	at Illinois	7	53,471
Oct. 6	41	Kansas State	0	50,841
Oct. 13	14	Oregon State (Portland)	13	30,030
Oct. 20	13	at Stanford	0	30,700
Oct. 27	21	Oregon	21	56,823
Nov. 3	0	at Southern Cal	14	46,456
Nov. 10	27	California	0	53,824
Nov. 17	30	UCLA	0	53,430
Nov. 24	26	WSU (Spokane)	21	35,494
Totals:	208		83	467,154

Co-Captains: Rod Scheyer, Bob Monroe

Honors

Guy Flaherty: Bob Monroe. **L. Walt Rising:** Rod Scheyer. **Brian Stapp:** Don Carnahan. **All-Coast:** Ray Mansfield, Rick Redman, Rod Scheyer, Junior Coffey.

Commentary

The Husky Rose Bowl hopes were dashed again by one game, a 14-0 loss at the hands of unbeaten National Champions, Southern California in Los Angeles. It was the only loss on the season for this outstanding team.

Lettermen

Andy Alkire	Glen Kezer	Gary Price
Lee Bernhardi	Jerry Knoll	Rick Redman
Mike Briggs	Jon Knoll	Joe Ryan
Charlie Browning	Jake Kupp	Don Safford
Don Carnahan	Duane Locknane	Rod Scheyer
Gary Clark	Ray Mansfield	Bill Siler
Junior Coffey	Charlie Mitchell	Rick Sortun
Norm Dicks	Bob Monroe	Jim Stiger
Bill Douglas	Jim Norton	John Stupey
Koll Hagen	Pete Ohler	Nat Whitmyer
Robbie Heinz	Dave Phillips	Martin Wyatt
Lynn Hewitt	John Piety	

1963

Record: 6-5		Finish: AAWU lst		Coach: Jim Owens
Date	UW	Opponent		Attendance
Sept. 21	7	at Air Force	10	23,542
Sept. 28	6	at Pittsburgh	13	27,136
Oct. 5	7	Iowa	17	55,942
Oct. 12	34	Oregon St.	7	55,827
Oct. 19	19	Stanford	11	54,213
Oct. 26	26	Oregon (Portland)	19	35,690
Nov. 2	22	Southern Cal	7	55,738
Nov. 9	39	at California	26	37,000
Nov. 16	0	at UCLA	14	30,398
Nov. 30	16	Washington State	0	57,300
Jan. 1	7	Illinois (Rose Bowl)	17	96,957
Totals:	183		141	527,743

Co-Captains: Dave Kopay, John Stupey

Honors

Guy Flaherty: Chuck Bond. **L. Walt Rising:** Mike Briggs. **Brian Stapp:** Brian Biggs.
All-American: Rick Redman. **All-Coast:** Rick Redman, Mike Briggs, Junior Coffey,

Commentary

This was a team that had a split personality: they lost their first three games of the season, then reeled off five straight wins against the strongest teams on their schedule. Then in Los Angeles against the weakest team on their schedule, they lost to a UCLA team which had won only one game all year, moreover, the Huskies were shut out, 14-0, for the first and only time all year. Nevertheless, the Huskies won the conference title and faced Illinois in the Rose Bowl. The hubris or split personality that seemed to dog this team followed them to Pasadena where a week before the Rose Bowl the team's leading rusher, Junior Coffey, broke his foot. Next with the game only half way through the first quarter, quarterback Bill Douglas sustained a serious knee injury. With their two best offensive threats out of the game it was too much for the Huskies to overcome and they lost to Illinois 17-7.

Lettermen

Chuck Bond	Steve Hinds	John O'Brien
Steve Bramwell	Dave Kopay	Mike Otis
Mike Briggs	Jerry Knoll	Rick Redman
Charles Browning	Jon Knoll	Joe Ryan
Junior Coffey	Jake Kupp	Don Safford
Bill Diehl	Jim Lambright	Jim Sampson
Bill Douglass	Al Libke	Rick Sortun
Fred Forsberg	Joe Mancuso	John Stupey
Koll Hagen	Ron Medved	Dick Wetterauer
Robbie Heinz	Jim Norton	Ralph Winters

1964

Record: 6-4		Finish: AAWU 3rd		Coach: Jim Owens	
Date	UW	Opponent			Attendance
Sept. 19	2	Air Force	3		57,201
Sept. 26	35	Baylor	14		57,302
Oct. 3	18	at Iowa	28		47,906
Oct. 10	7	Oregon St. (Portland)	9		33,853
Oct. 17	6	at Stanford	0		30,468
Oct. 24	0	Oregon	7		55,625
Oct. 31	14	at Southern Cal	13		47,906
Nov. 7	21	California	16		55,893
Nov. 14	22	UCLA	20		54,264
Nov. 21	14	Wash. St. (Spokane)	0		57,300
Totals:	139		110		474.053

Co-Captains: Rick Redman, Charlie Browning

Honors

Guy Flaherty: Jim Lambright. **L. Walt Rising:** Rick Redman. **Brian Stapp:** Keith Cordes. **All-American:** Rick Redman. **All-Coast:** Rick Redman, Jim Lambright, Koll Hagen, Jim Norton.

Commentary

With many veterans returning from the Rose Bowl team the Huskies were overwhelming pre-season favorites to repeat as conference champions and return to Pasadena. This was the first year of a NCAA rule change returning to two platoon football. The change in rules seemed a puzzle to this team from the very first game as they lost the home opener by a baseball score of 3-2 to Air Force. That set the tone for the season and this team never found itself finishing with a disappointing record of 6 wins and 4 loses. The problem, as in the past, was offense. But the defense lead the nation in rushing defense and placed four players on the All-Coast defensive team. Rick Redman became the first Husky player to be named All-Coast in all three years of his eligibility.

Lettermen

Bill Barnes	Tod Hullin	Omar Parker
Steve Bramwell	Jeff Jordan	Rick Redman
Gary Brandt	Jerry Knoll	Mike Ryan
Charlie Browning	Jon Knoll	Jim Sampson
Gary Carr	Bruce Kramer	Jim Sartoris
Junior Coffey	Jim Lambright	Paul Scheyer
Bill Douglass	Al Libke	Dale Stephens
Roger Dunn	Ron Medved	Mike Stroud
Fred Forsberg	Mason Mitchell	Dick Wetterauer
Tom Greenlee	Jim Norton	Dave Williams
Koll Hagen	Lyle Norwood	Jerry Williams
Robbie Heinz	Mike O'Bannon	Ralph Winters
Steve Hinds	Mike Otis	

1965

Record: 5-5		Finish: AAWU 4th		Coach: Jim Owens
Date	UW	Opponent		Attendance
Sept. 18	14	Idaho	9	54,682
Sept. 25	14	at Baylor	17	22,000
Oct. 2	21	Ohio State	23	54,132
Oct. 9	0	Southern Cal	34	57,533
Oct. 16	12	at California	16	35,000
Oct. 23	24	Oregon (Portland)	20	33,437
Oct. 30	41	Stanford	8	50,633
Nov. 6	24	at UCLA	28	46,084
Nov. 13	28	Oregon State	21	53,187
Nov. 20	27	Washington State	9	57,395
Totals:	205		185	464,083

Co-Captains: Ron Medved, Ralph Winters

Honors

Guy Flaherty: Ron Medved. **L. Walt Rising:** Fred Forsberg. **Brian Stapp:** John Davis. **All-Coast:** Fred Forsberg, Dave Williams, Tom Greenlee

Commentary

Like the last two Husky teams this was an up and down outfit sometimes displaying briliance and at other times struggling with mediocrity. The brilliance of receiver Dave Williams was put on display at UCLA where he caught 10 passes for 257 and three touchdowns, which is still a Husky record. The game became infamous for what became known at the "Z-streak" where a UCLA player pretended to be standing on the sidelines out of bounds and then as the ball was snapped ran toward the endzone to receive a touchdown pass - which decided the game in favor of UCLA 28-24 and propelled them toward a Rose Bowl rematch with unbeaten Michigan State.

Lettermen

Bill Barnes	Dean Halverson	Mike Otis
John Beymer	Steve Hinds	Omar Parker
Mac Bledsoe	Tod Hullin	Bob Pederson
Steve Bramwell	Jeff Jordan	Bob Richardson
Gary Brandt	Jim Kirk	Mike Ryan
Gary Carr	Bruce Kramer	Dale Stephens
Greg Cass	Al Libke	Bill Stifter
Ron Clark	Vince Lorrain	Steve Thompson
Dave Dillon	Joe Mancuso	Dick Wetterauer
Dave Dinish	Don Martin	Dave Williams
Roger Dunn	Rick McHale	Jerry Williams
Fred Forsberg	Ron Medved	Ralph Winters
Bill Glennon	Don Moore	
Tom Greenlee	Lyle Norwood	

1966

Record: 6-4		Finish: AAWU 4th		Coach: Jim Owens
Date	**UW**	**Opponent**		**Attendance**
Sept. 17	19	Idaho	7	55,360
Sept. 24	0	Air Force	10	56,110
Oct. 1	38	at Ohio State	22	80,241
Oct. 8	14	at Southern Cal	17	55,960
Oct. 15	20	California	24	54,112
Oct. 22	10	Oregon	7	50,596
Oct. 29	22	at Stanford	20	38,500
Nov. 5	16	UCLA	3	55,536
Nov. 12	13	at Oregon State	24	21,347
Nov. 19	19	at Washington State	7	33,800
Totals:	**171**		**141**	**501,562**

Co-Captains: Tom Greenlee, Mike Ryan

Honors

Guy Flaherty: Jeff Jordan. **L. Walt Rising:** Tom Greenlee. **Brian Stapp:** Clarence Pautzke. **All-America:** Tom Greenlee. **All-Coast:** Tom Greenlee, Dave Williams,

Commentary

This Husky edition finished with a 6-4 mark, once again stuck at mid-level in the conference. The outstandng performance of the year was by junior running back Donnie Moore who rushed for 221 yards to spark an upset over Ohio State in Columbus and the next week was dismissed from the team for "violating team rules".

Lettermen

Bob Anderson
Bill Barnes
Mac Bledsoe
Gary Brandt
Greg Cass
Cliff Coker
Jim Cope
Dave Dillon
Dave Dupree
Bill Glennon
Tom Greenlee
Dean Halverson
Ron Hudson
Jeff Huget

Larry Jakl
Vince Janowicz
Jeff Jordan
George Jugum
Jim Kirk
Vince Lorrain
Mike Maggart
Don Martin
Jim McCabe
Rick McHale
Bill Parker
Omar Parker
Bob Pederson
Bob Richardson

Mike Ryan
Steve Sanford
Jim Sartoris
Avery Schwartz
Frank Smith
Tom Sparlin
Dan Spriesterbach
Steve Thompson
Gerald Wea
Dave Williams
Jerry Williams
Harrison Wood
Al Worley

1967

Record: 5-5		Finish: AAWU 4th		Coach: Jim Owens
Date	**UW**	**Opponent**		**Attendance**
Sept. 16	7	Nebraska	17	57,481
Sept. 23	17	Wisconsin	0	54,564
Sept. 30	30	at Air Force	7	34,739
Oct. 7	13	Oregon State	6	56,033
Oct. 14	26	at Oregon	0	33,500
Oct. 21	6	Southern Cal	23	58,754
Oct. 28	23	at California	6	30,000
Nov. 4	7	Stanford	14	52,048
Nov. 11	0	at UCLA	48	46,368
Nov. 25	7	Washington State	9	49,041
Totals:	**136**		**130**	**472,528**

Co-Captains: Mac Bledsoe, Dean Halverson, Steve Thompson.

Honors

Guy Flaherty: Cliff Coker. **L. Walt Rising:** Dean Halverson. **Brian Stapp:** Les Dicks.
All-Coast: Steve Thompson, Dean Halverson

Commnetary

The record, both wins and loses as well as scores best describes this team. Mediocre in every way.

Lettermen

Bob Anderson	Gary James	Frank Smith
Ken Ballenger	Vince Janowicz	Tom Sparlin
Bob Berg	George Jugum	Dan Spriesterbach
Harvey Blanks	Ken Lee	Bill Sprinkle
Mac Bledsoe	Mike Maggart	Steve Thompson
Lee Brock	Tom Manke	Tom Verti
Cliff Coker	Don Martin	Otis Washington
Jim Cope	Jim McCabe	Gerald Wea
Dave Dupree	Rick McHale	Clyde Werner
Roger Flewelling	Bob Pederson	Carl Wojciechowski
Bill Glennon	Dave Plumely	Harrison Wood
Dean Halverson	Bob Richardson	Al Worley
Jim Harris	Augie Rios	Dick Zatkovich
Ron Hudson	Bob Schoepper	
Jeff Huget	Rick Sharp	

1968

Record: 3-5-2		Finish: PAC-8 8th		Coach: Jim Owens
Date	UW	Opponent		Attendance
Sept. 21	35	Rice	35	50,038
Sept. 28	21	at Wisconsin	17	42,965
Oct. 5	21	at Oregon State	35	30,220
Oct. 12	0	Oregon	3	52,737
Oct. 19	7	at Southern Cal	14	60,990
Oct. 26	37	Idaho	7	49,538
Nov. 2	7	California	7	50,266
Nov. 9	20	at Stanford	35	33,000
Nov. 16	6	UCLA	0	52,500
Nov. 23	0	at Washington State	24	31,986
Totals:	154		177	454,240

Co-Captains: Jim Cope, Al Worley

Honors

Guy Flaherty: Cliff Coker. **L. Walt Rising:** Dean Halverson. **Brian Stapp:** Les Dicks. **All-American:** Al Worley. **All-Coast:** Al Worley, George Jugum.

Commentary

The old AAWU conference died and for the first time since 1958 Oregon, Oregon State, and Washington State rejoined the conference under the new name Pacific-Eight conference. But the Huskies stumbled their way to an eighth place in the new conference posting a lackluster 1-5-1 record. The highlight of this season was the performance of defensive back Al Worley. Worley set an NCAA recod by intercepting 14 passes during the season. His career 18 inteceptions are still a Husky record. For his efforts Worley was named to numerous All-American teams and given the nickname *The Thief* for his uncanny ability to steal passes.

Lettermen

Bob Anderson	Ernie Janet	Avery Schwartz
Ken Ballenger	Bruce Jarvis	Rick Sharp
Bob Berg	George Jugum	Wayne Sortun
Harvey Blanks	Jerry Kaloper	Dan Spriesterbach
Lee Brock	Buddy Kennamer	Bill Sprinkle
Alan Bulger	Ken Lee	Mark Turner
Jim Cope	Bob Lovelien	Tom Verti
Bo Cornell	Mike Maggart	Ron Volbrecht
Tom Failla	Tom Manke	Otis Washington
Mark Hannah	Dave McClinton	Barry Wegner
Jim Harris	Lamar Mills	Clyde Werner
Jeff Huget	Augie Rios	Carl Wojciechowski
Dennis Hurley	Lane Ronnebaum	Harrison Wood
Gary James	Bob Schoepper	Al Worley

1969

Date	UW	Opponent		Attendance
		Record: 1-9-0	**Finish:** PAC-8 7th	**Coach:** Jim Owens
Sept. 20	11	at Michigan State	27	63,022
Sept. 27	7	at Michigan	45	49,684
Oct. 4	14	Ohio State	41	57,150
Oct. 11	13	at California	44	34,000
Oct. 18	6	Oregon State	10	53,824
Oct. 25	7	at Oregon	22	34,200
Nov. 1	14	at UCLA	57	34,899
Nov. 8	7	Stanford	21	50,976
Nov. 15	7	Southern Cal	16	51,403
Nov. 22	30	Washington State	21	55,677
Totals:	**116**		**304**	**454,240**

Co-Captains: Ken Ballenger, Lee Brock

Honors

Guy Flaherty: Lee Brock. **L. Walt Rising:** Mark Hannah. **Brian Stapp:** Loren Brucker. **All-Coast:** Lee Brock.

Commentary

If ever was a there was a season Husky fans would like to forget this was it. Coach Owens installed a modified version of the popular wishbone offense in the spring, but it never got off the ground, although fullback Bo Cornell was effective at fullback and rushed for 147 yards in a losing effort against Southern Cal. There was also racial turmoil in the program.

Lettermen

Cal Allen
Ken Ballenger
Rank Baty
Ralph Bayard
Joe Bell
Bob Berg
Lee Brock
Alan Bulger
Bob Burmeister
Gary Carr
Bo Cornell
Alan Craig
Dan Cunningham
Mark Day
Tom Failla
Rob Fink

Dick Galuska
John Garland
Dan Gosselin
Mark Hannah
Steve Hanzlik
Jim Harris
Herman Houston
Rick Huget
Ernie Janet
Bruce Jarvis
Jon Kadletz
Rick Keely
Buddy Kennamer
Bob Lovelien
Al Mauer
Mark McMahon

Bob Middleton
Tom Nelson
Ron Preston
Augie Rios
Lane Ronnebaum
Don Roberson
Rick Sharp
Luther Sligh
Wayner Sortun
Carl Sweet
Tom Verti
Ron Volbrecht
Clyde Werner
Gene Willis

1970

Date	UW	Opponent		Attendance
Record: 6-4-0		Finish: PAC-8 Tie 2nd	Coach:	Jim Owens
Sept. 19	42	Michigan State	16	52,240
Sept. 26	3	Michigan	17	56,106
Oct. 3	56	Navy	7	55,292
Oct. 10	28	California	31	53,240
Oct. 17	25	at Southern Cal (night)	28	56,166
Oct. 24	29	at Oregon State	20	27,911
Oct. 31	25	Oregon	23	58,580
Nov. 7	22	at Stanford	29	59,066
Nov. 14	61	UCLA	20	59,208
Nov. 21	43	at Washington State	25	33,200
Totals:	334		216	511,189

Co-Captains: Bo Cornell, Tom Failla.

Honors

Guy Flaherty: Tom Failla. L. Walt Rising: Ernie Janet, Bob Jarvis, Tom Failla. Brian Stapp: Mike Wilds. All-Coast: Ernie Janet, Tom Failla, Calvin Jones.

Commentary

An unknown sophomore quarterback, Sonny Sixkiller, took his first snap from center in 1970. Sixkiller brought back to Husky Stadium excitement. There was a feeling as long as he was throwing passes every game was winable. And for the next three years it almost always was.

Lettermen

Ben Albrecht
Rank Baty
Ralph Bayard
Joe Bell
John Brady
Ace Bulger
Bob Burmeister
Bill Cahill
Gary Carr
Randy Coleman
Greg Collins
Bo Cornell
Al Craig
Dan Cunningham
Darrell Downey
Roy Easton

Dave Enders
Tom Failla
Bob Ferguson
Dick Galuska
Gordy Guinn
Ira Hammon
Rick Hays
Dennis Hurley
Ernie Janet
Bruce Jarvis
Calvin Jones
Jim Katsenes
Al Kravitz
Jim Krieg
Ken Lee
Bob Lovelien

Kurt Matter
Al Mauer
Mark McMahon
Fred Miller
Ron Preson
Lane Ronnebaum
Steve Schulte
Ron Shepherd
Sonny Sixkiller
Wayne Sortun
Dick Sweat
Mark Turner
Ron Volbrecht
Steve Wiezbowski
Dave Worgan
Larry Worley

1971

Record: 8-3-0		Finish: PAC-8 3rd		Coach: Jim Owens	
Date	**UW**	**Opponent**			**Attendance**
Sept. 11	65	U.C. Santa Barbara	7		56,180
Sept. 18	38	Purdue	35		55,927
Sept. 25	44	Texas Christian	26		59,956
Oct. 2	52	at Illinois	14		48,127
Oct. 9	6	Stanford	17		60,777
Oct. 16	21	at Oregon	23		44,220
Oct. 23	38	Oregon State	14		60,404
Oct. 30	23	at UCLA	12		36,545
Nov. 6	30	at California	7		36,000
Nov. 13	12	Southern Cal	13		59.082
Nov. 20	28	Washington State	20		60,497
Totals:	**357**		**188**		**581,595**

Co-Captains: Steve Anderson, Rick Huget, Al Kravitz, Sonny Sixkiller.

Honors

Guy Flaherty: Al Kravitz. **L. Walt Rising:** Al Kravitz, Steve Anderson, Gordy Guinn.
Brian Stapp: Rick Simpson. **All-Coast:** Calvin Jones, Tom Scott

Commentary

Another Sixkiller edition continued the excitement in Husky Stadium, but three conference loses kept the Huskies in Seattle and not in Pasadena for the holidays.

Lettermen

Ben Albrecht	Pete Elswick	Fred Miller
Steve Anderson	Dave Enders	Dain Rodwell
Phil Andre	Bob Ferguson	Tom Roehl
Jim Andrilenas	Dick Galuska	Steve Schulte
Tony Apostle	Don Gorman	Tom Scott
Tony Bonwell	Dan Gosselin	Sonny Sixkiller
John Brady	Gordy Guinn	Luther Sligh
Dennis Brimhall	Rick Hays	Rod Stanely
Charlie Buckland	Rick Huget	Dick Sweat
Bill Cahill	Jerry Ingals	Pete Taggares
Randy Coleman	Calvin Jones	Tom Tymer
Greg Collins	Washington Keenan	Steve Wallin
Al Craig	Al Kelso	Jerry Watts
Mark Day	Al Kravitz	Steve Wiezbowski
Brian Doheny	Jim Kreig	Dave Worgan
Larry Dumas	Scott Loomis	
Jim Eicher	Kurt Matter	

1972

| Record: 8-3-0 | | Finish: PAC-8 Tie 3rd | | Coach: Jim Owens |
Date	UW	Opponent		Attendance
Sept. 9	13	Pacific	6	57,500
Sept. 16	14	Duke	6	59,200
Sept. 23	22	at Purdue	21	60,102
Sept. 30	31	Illinois	11	60,200
Oct. 7	23	Oregon	17	61,000
Oct. 14	0	at Stanford	24	56,000
Oct. 21	7	at Southern Cal	34	59,151
Oct. 28	35	California	21	56,300
Nov. 4	23	at Oregon State	16	31,923
Nov. 11	30	UCLA	21	59.000
Nov. 18	10	at Washington State	27	34,100
Totals:	208		204	594,476

Co-Captains: Bill Cahill, Sonny Sixkiller

Honors

Guy Flaherty: Calvin Jones. L. Walt Rising: Al Kelson, Gordy Guinn, Kurt Matter. Brian Stapp: Al McIlheney. All-American: Calvin Jones. All-Coast: Calvin Jones, Gordy Guinn.

Commentary

In Sonny Sixkiller's last chance to guide the Huskies into the Rose Bowl two old nemeses returned: Stanford and Southern Cal. The Huskies played both on the road and were overwhelmed by both in back to back games. The rest of the season was anti-climatic and ended with a thud in Spokane and a 27-10 shellacking at the hands of the Cougars.

Lettermen

Ben Albrecht	Calvin Jones	Tom Scott
Phil Andre	Roberto Jordan	Ron Shepherd
Glen Bonner	Washington Keenan	Sonny Sixkiller
Tony Bonwell	Al Kelso	Luther Sligh
John Brady	Jim Kristof	Jim Smith
Bill Cahill	Dan Lloyd	Joe Tabor
Brian Doheny	Scott Loomis	Pete Taggares
Darrell Downey	Kurt Matter	Steve Wallin
Pete Elswick	Murphy McFarland	Don Wesley
Dave Enders	Fred Miller	John Whitacre
Bob Ferguson	Walter Oldes	Steve Wiezbowski
Don Gorman	Dave Pear	Hans Woldseth
Gordy Guinn	Tom Roehl	Dave Worgan
Barry Houlihan	Steve Schulte	

1973

Record: 2-9-0		Finish: PAC-8 8th		Coach: Jim Owens
Date	**UW**	**Opponent**		**Attendance**
Sept. 15	7	Hawaii	10	52,250
Sept. 22	21	at Duke	23	22,500
Sept. 29	21	Syracuse	7	54,500
Oct. 6	49	at California	54	28,000
Oct. 13	7	Oregon State	31	55,000
Oct. 20	14	Stanford	23	51,500
Oct. 27	0	at Oregon	58	40,000
Nov. 3	13	at UCLA	62	30,000
Nov. 10	41	Idaho	14	50,000
Nov. 17	19	Southern Cal	42	55,500
Nov. 24	26	Washington State	52	56,500
Totals:	**218**		**376**	**496,000**

Co-Captains: Joe Andrilenas, Washington Keenan, Joe Tabor, John Whitacre

Honors

Guy Flaherty: Jim Andrilenas. **L. Walt Rising:** Ray Phinney, Walter Olds, Dave Pear. **Brian Stapp:** Kirk Hawkins. **All-Coast:** Dave Pear.

Commentary

To say this was a rebuilding year was a bit of an understatement: the defense surrendered points by the bucket fulls. Southern Cal rang up 42, Washington State 52, Cal 54, Oregon 58, and UCLA broke the bank with 62. Enough said.

Lettermen

Jim Anderson	Rick Hayes	Jim Pettigrew
Jim Andrilenas	Willie Hendricks	Scott Phillips
Glen Bonner	Charles Jackson	Ray Pinney
Bob Bousted	Roberto Jordan	Lou Quinn
Skip Boyd	Washington Keenan	Frank Reed
Reggie Brown	Mark Kretuz	Carl Rose
Al Burleson	Jim Kristof	Chris Rowland
Dan Celoni	Steve Lipe	Dean Schlamp
Ken Conely	Dan Lloyd	Rod Stanely
Mike Dochow	Clifton Marcus	Paul Strohmeier
Brian Doheny	Bob Martin	Joe Tabor
Robin Earl	Mark McDonald	Pete Taggares
Pete Elswick	Murphy McFarland	Donnie T. Waters
Denny Fitzpatrick	Wayne Moses	John Whitacre
Bob Graves	Walter Oldes	Hans Woldseth
Mike Green	Dave Pear	
Pedro Hawkins	Nelse Petermann	

1974

Record: 5-6-0		Finish: PAC-8 Tie 5th		Coach: Jim Owens
Date	**UW**	**Opponent**		**Attendance**
Sept. 14	21	Cincinnati	17	47,000
Sept. 21	31	Iowa State	28	47,500
Sept. 28	15	Texas A & M	28	54,000
Oct. 5	21	at Texas	35	50,250
Oct. 12	9	at Oregon State	23	26,951
Oct. 19	17	at Stanford	34	38,000
Oct. 26	66	Oregon	0	52,500
Nov. 2	31	UCLA	9	52,000
Nov. 9	26	California	52	54,500
Nov. 16	11	at Southern Cal	42	51,157
Nov. 23	24	at Washington State	17	27,800
Totals:	**272**		**285**	**507,658**

Co-Captains: Willie Hendricks, Bob Martin, Dave Pear, Ray Pinney.

Honors

Guy Flaherty: Dennis Fitzpatrick. **L. Walt Rising:** Ray Phinney, Charles Jackson, Dave Pear. **Brian Stapp:** Steve Sly, Guy Marquiss.

Commentary

The 1974 edition not only defeated three teams which had blew them out the year before, but they got some revenge in the process. Oregon which had beaten the Huskies 58-0 in 73', took it on the chin in Husky Stadium 66-0, UCLA which had stomped the Huskies 62-13 in 73' got rolled over in Seattle 31-9, and Washington State which had cruised over Washington 52-26 in 73', got slugged 24-17. In the Washington State game quarterback Denny Fitzpatrick rushed for 249 yards which remains a record for Husky quarterbacks. After 18 seasons as Husky coach, Jim Owens resigned.

Lettermen

Jim Anderson	Pedro Hawkins	Scott Phillips
Mike Baldassin	Willie Hendricks	Ray Pinney
Paul Bianchini	Charles Jackson	Lou Quinn
Bob Boustead	Roberto Jourdan	Eddie Ray
Skip Boyd	Mark Kreutz	Frank Reed
Reggie Brown	Jim Kristof	Steve Robbins
Al Burleson	Steve Lipe	Chris Rowland
Dan Celoni	Dan Lloyd	Eugene Sanders
Corny Chenevert	Dave Lutes	Dean Schlamp
Ken Conley	Clifton Marcus	Greg Smith
Fred Dean	Bob Martin	Paul Strohmeier
Robin Earl	Mark McDonald	Carl VanValkenberg
Denny Fitzpatrick	Wayne Moses	Mike Vicino
Rob Gehring	Ron Olson	Don Wardlow
Bob Graves	Mike Oswald	Dee Washington
Mike Green	Dave Pear	
Rusty Gregory	Nelse Petermann	

1975

Record: 6-5-0		Finish: PAC-8 Tie 3rd		Coach: Don James	
Date	UW	Opponent			Attendance
Sept. 13	12	at Arizona State (night)	35		50,194
Sept. 20	10	Texas	28		56,000
Sept. 27	14	Navy	13		53,000
Oct. 4	27	at Oregon	17		28,500
Oct. 11	0	at Alabama	52		58,000
Oct. 18	21	Stanford	24		45,000
Oct. 25	35	Oregon State	7		43,500
Nov. 1	17	at UCLA	13		29,158
Nov. 8	24	at California	27		43,270
Nov. 15	8	Southern Cal	7		53,700
Nov. 22	28	Washington State	27		57,100
Totals:	196		250		517,422

Co-Captains: Ray Pinney, John Whitacre, Dan Lloyd, Al Burleson

Honors

Guy Flaherty: Dan Lloyd. **L. Walt Rising:** Ray Phinney, Dan Lloyd, John Whitacre, Paul Strohmeier. **Brian Stapp:** John Edwards. **All-Coast:** Al Burleson, Ray Pinney, Dan Lloyd.

Commentary

New Husky coach, Don James from Kent State of Ohio, first team lost their first game at Arizona State 35-12 and also lost 52-0 at Alabama. But they regrouped to beat both UCLA and Southern Cal, the first time the Huskies had defeated both in one season since 1964. The best, however, was saved for the last game against WSU: *the Miracle Finish.* Trailing 24-13 with barely over two minutes remaining, and WSU threatening near the Husky goal line, the Huskies scored two touchdowns and won 28-27.

Lettermen

James Anderson	Scott Greenwood	Frank Reed
Mike Baldassin	Rusty Gregory	Kevin Richardson
Dave Belmondo	Pedro Hawkins	Steve Robbins
Paul Bianchini	Frank Hemphill	Mike Rohrbach
Gordy Bronson	Charles Jackson	Chris Rowland
Greg Brooks	Mike Jackson	Dean Schlamp
Al Burleson	Roberto Jourdan	Joe Simmons
Blair Bush	Mark Kreutz	Paul Strohmeier
Dan Celoni	Steve Lipe	Dave Stromswold
Craig Davillier	Dan Lloyd	Jeff Toews
Randy Earl	Dave Lutes	Lou Quinn
Robin Earl	Guy Marquiss	Carl VanValkenberg
Don Feleay	Greg Martin	Mike Vicino
Robert Gains	Warren Moon	Stan Walderhaug
Willy Galoia	Mike Nykreim	Don Wardlow
Leon Garrett	Ron Olson	Roger Westlund
Robert Gehrig	Nelse Petermann	John Whitacre
Nesby Glasgow	Scott Phillips	Stan Wilson
Bob Graves	Ray Pinney	
Mike Green	Eddie Ray	

1976

Record: 5-6-0		Finish: PAC-8 Tie 4th		Coach: Don James
Date	UW	Opponent		Attendance
Sept. 11	38	Virginia	17	40,412
Sept. 18	7	Colorado	21	43,383
Sept. 25	13	Indiana	20	40,425
Oct. 2	38	Minnesota	7	40,694
Oct. 9	24	at Oregon State	12	27,096
Oct. 16	28	at Stanford	34	36,000
Oct. 23	14	Oregon	7	43,129
Oct. 30	21	UCLA	30	47,187
Nov. 6	0	California	7	42,932
Nov. 13	3	at Southern Cal	20	49,264
Nov. 20	51	at Washington State	32	35,800
Totals:	237		207	446,322

Co-Captains: Robin Earl, Charles Jackson, Scott Phillips, Mike Baldassin.

Honors

Guy Flaherty: Mike Baldassin. **L. Walt Rising:** Carl Van Valkenberg, Charles Jackson. **Brian Stapp:** Steve Cupic. **Bob Jarvis:** Dean Brooke. **All-Coast:** Charles Jackson.

Commentary

This was a kind of shake down year when Don James installed more of his program and brought in several key recruits, such as quarterback Warren Moon. The results were unspectacular, but the fundamentals of the system were put in place which would, sooner than most expected, pay surprising dividends.

Lettermen

Duane Akina	Ron Gipson	Scott Phillips
Mike Baldassin	Nesby Glasgow	Ant. Richardson
Dean Brooke	Scott Greenwood	Kevin Richardson
Greg Brooks	Bruce Harrell	Steve Robbins
Dave Browning	Kyle Heinrich	Wayne Roche
Blair Bush	Charles Jackson	Ron Rowland
Dan Chavira	Mike Jackson	Joe Sanford
Marshall Cromer	Bob Johanson	Terry Sherwood
Tony Cuesta	Frank Jones	Rob Smith
Robin Earl	John Kerley	Joe Steele
John Edwards	Dave Labrousse	Dave Stromswold
Don Feleay	Doug Martin	Lance Theoudele
Phil Foreman	Cliff McBride	Jeff Toews
Bret Gagliardi	Warren Moon	Carl VanValkenberg
Robert Gains	Rudy Moraga	Stan Walderhaug
Willy Galoia	Wayne Moses	Don Wardlow
Leon Garrett	Rick Noeltner	Roger Westlund
Rob Gehring	Vern Olson	Stan Wilson

1977

Record: 7-4-0		Finish: PAC-8 1st		Coach: Don James	
Date	**UW**	**Opponent**			**Attendance**
Sept. 10	18	Mississippi State	27		45,050
Sept. 17	24	San Jose State	3		36,489
Sept. 24	20	at Syracuse	22		12,839
Oct. 1	17	at Minnesota	19		31,895
Oct. 8	54	at Oregon	0		29,500
Oct. 15	45	Stanford	21		45,529
Oct. 22	14	Oregon State	6		46,677
Oct. 29	21	at UCLA	30		47,187
Nov. 5	50	at California	31		38,812
Nov. 12	28	Southern Cal	10		59,901
Nov. 19	35	Washington State	15		60,964
Jan. 2	27	Michigan (Rose Bowl)	20		105,312
Totals:	**344**		**194**		**552,260**

Co-Captains: Dave Browning, Blair Bush, Mike Rohrbach, Warren Moon.   .

Honors

Guy Flaherty: Warren Moon. **L. Walt Rising:** Dave Browning, Jeff Towes. **Brian Stapp:** Dean Perryman. **Bob Jarvis:** Mark Passinetti. **All-American:** Jeff Toews. **All-Coast:** Dave Browning, Blair Bush, Nesby Glasgow, Michael Jackson.

Commentary

This team started slowly and after four games seemed lost at sea with a 1-3 record, then exploded against Oregon in Eugene. Only a loss at UCLA prevented a perfect conference record. In Pasadena the team played its best game of the year to upset Michigan.

Lettermen

Duane Akina	Ron Grant	Steve Robbins
Steve Bauer	Scott Greenwood	Wayne Roche
Micheal Bean	Greg Grimes	Mike Rohrbach
Cliff Beathea	Bruce Harrell	Ron Rowland
Gary Briggs	Kyle Heinrich	Trip Rumberger
Gregg Brooks	Michael Jackson	Terry Sherwood
Dave Browning	Doug Kerly	Bob Smith
Blair Bush	Mark Lee	Joe Steele
Dan Chavira	Jeff Leeland	Kyle Stevens
Marshall Cromer	Scot Long	Lance Theoudele
Steve Cupic	Curt Marsh	Jeff Toews
Mike Curtis	Doug Martin	Pete Tormey
John Edwards	Jerry McLain	Tom Turnure
Phil Foreman	Warren Moon	Toussaint Tyler
Bret Gagliardi	Rudy Moraga	Stan Walderhaug
Robert Gains	Wayne Moses	Don Wardlow
Willy Galoia	Jim Pence	Roger Westlund
Ron Gipson	Ant. Richardson	Aaron Wilson
Nesby Glasgow	Keith Richardson	

1978

| Record: 7-4-0 | | Finish: PAC-10 Tie 2nd | | Coach: Don James |
Date	UW	Opponent		Attendance
Sept. 9	7	UCLA	10	55,780
Sept. 16	31	Kansas	2	49,624
Sept. 23	7	at Indiana	14	40,244
Sept. 30	34	at Oregon State	0	30,000
Oct. 7	17	Alabama	20	60,975
Oct. 14	34	at Stanford	31	58,079
Oct. 21	20	Oregon	14	49,602
Oct. 28	41	Arizona State	7	54,866
Nov. 4	31	Arizona	21	47,587
Nov. 11	10	at Southern Cal	28	54,071
Nov. 18	38	at Washington State	8	35,187
Totals:	270		155	571,202

Co-Captains: Michael Jackson, Nesby Glasgow, Jeff Toews, Scott Greenwood.

Honors

Guy Flaherty: Michael Jackson. **L. Walt Rising:** Jeff Towes, Doug Martin. **Brian Stapp:** Bill Stapleton. **Bob Jarvis:** Curtis Cummings. **All-American:** Jeff Toews, Micheal Jackson, Doug Martin. **All-Coast:** Jeff Toews, Michael Jackson, Nesby Glasgow, Doug Martin.

Commentary

Hopes were high with many key players returning from the Rose Bowl team which had upset Michigan, but the old proverb about *uneasy rests the head on which the crown rests* proved to be prophetic as Washington's old nemesis UCLA upset the Huskies in the opening game 10-7. The 1978 Huskies played catch up to Southern Cal the whole season only to finish second.

Lettermen

Duane Akina	Kyle Heinrich	Ant. Richardson
Steve Bauer	Michael Jackson	Keith Richardson
Ron Blacken	John Kerley	Wayne Roche
Gary Briggs	Mike Lansford	Joe Sanford
Dan Chavira	Mark Lee	Calvin Saunders
Vince Coby	Jeff Leeland	Rob Smith
Marshall Cromer	Chris Linnin	Joe Steele
Phil Foreman	Brent Mackie	Kyle Stevens
Bret Gagliardi	Curtis Marsh	Lance Theoudele
Spider Gaines	Doug Martin	Jeff Toews
Willy Galoia	Stafford Mays	Pete Tormey
Ken Gardner	Jerry McLain	Tom Turnure
Ron Gipson	Rudy Moraga	Toussaint Tyler
Nesby Glasgow	Grge. Papageorgiou	Randy Van Divier
Scott Greenwood	Jim Pence	Roger Westlund
Greg Grimes	Steve Pope	Aaron Wilson
Bruce Harrell	Tom Porras	Ron Wold

1979

Record: 10-2-0		**Finish:** PAC-10 2nd		**Coach:** Don James
Date	**UW**	**Opponent**		**Attendance**
Sept. 8	38	Wyoming	2	47,530
Sept. 15	41	Utah	7	49,735
Sept. 22	21	at Oregon	17	42,500
Sept. 29	49	Fresno State	14	47,376
Oct. 6	41	Oregon State	0	49,881
Oct. 13	7	at Arizona State* (night)	12	70,912
Oct. 20	14	Pittsburgh	26	52,485
Oct. 27	34	at UCLA	14	35,757
Nov. 3	28	at California	24	25,000
Nov. 10	17	Southern Cal	24	60,527
Nov. 17	17	Washington St.	7	56,110
Dec. 22	14	Texas (Sun Bowl)	7	33,412
Totals:	**321**		**154**	**571,225**

Co-Captains: Phil Foreman, Doug Martin, Joe Steele, Antowaine Richardson. *Forfeit - ineligible player.

Honors

Guy Flaherty: Joe Steele. **L. Walt Rising:** Tom Tunure, Bruce Harrel. **Brian Stapp:** John Gardenhire. **Bob Jarvis:** Curtis Cummings. **All-American:** Doug Martin, Mark Lee. **All-Coast:** Doug Martin, Mark Lee, Tom Tunure, Bruce Harrell, Joe Steele.

Commentary

After a mid-season embarrassment against Pittsburgh, Tom Flick is named the starting quarterback and the teams cruises from there. A sour note, Senior running back Joe Steel, who broke the school career rushing record, is injured late in the season against - who else - UCLA.

Lettermen

Anthony Allen	Ray Horton	Keith Richardson
David Bayle	Fletcher Jenkins	Joe Sanford
Ron Blacken	Mark Jerue	Joel Schmit
Gary Briggs	Clifton Johnson	Terry Sherwood
Dennis Brown	Mike Lansford	Phil Skansi
Tom Burnham	Mark Lee	Chris Smith
Rich Camarillo	Chris Linnin	Bill Stapleton
Randy Carrothers	Curt Marsh	Joe Steele
Dan Chavira	Doug Martin	Kyle Stevens
David Clawson	Stafford Mays	Mark Stewart
Vince Coby	Jerry McLain	Lance Theoudele
James Davis	Rudy Moraga	Pete Tormey
Don Dow	Lance Neubauer	Tom Turnure
Ken Driscoll	Vince Newsome	Toussaint Tyler
Tom Flick	Chris O'Connor	Randy Van Divier
Phil Foreman	Rusty Olsen	Doug Weston
Ken Gardner	Mike Pederson	Ron Wheeler
Ron Gipson	Jim Pence	Aaron Williams
Greg Grimes	Tom Porras	Greg Williams
Bruce Harrell	Mike Reilly	
Derek Harvey	Ant. Richardson	

1980

Record: 9-3-0		Finish: PAC-10 lst		Coach: Don James
Date	**UW**	**Opponent**		**Attendance**
Sept. 13	50	Air Force	7	44,999
Sept. 20	45	Northwestern	7	49,975
Sept. 27	10	Oregon	34	56,282
Oct. 4	24	at Oklahoma State	18	48,200
Oct. 11	41	at Oregon State	6	33,000
Oct. 18	27	at Stanford	24	60,066
Oct. 25	10	Navy	24	48,841
Nov. 1	25	Arizona State	0	48,691
Nov. 8	45	Arizona	0	49,341
Nov. 15	20	at Southern Cal	10	55,512
Nov. 22	30	at Washington St.	23	34,557
Jan.1	6	Michigan (Rose Bowl)	23	104,863
Totals:	**333**		**198**	**634,347**

Co-Captains: Tom Flick, Ken Gardner, Rusty Olsen, Randy Van Divier.

Honors

Guy Flaherty: Tom Flick. **L. Walt Rising:** Curt Marsh, Randy Van Divier, Mark Jerue. **Brian Stapp:** Ralph Parks **Bob Jarvis:** Stewart Keyes. **All-Coast:** Chuck Nelson.

Commentary

This was an up and down edition of Huskies. After winning impressively their first two games of the season they got steam rolled at home by Oregon 34-10, then lost again at home 24-10 to a so-so Navy team at the midway point in the season. Then turned around to record back to back shutouts over Arizona State and Arizona, trumping that with two road winds over Southern Cal and Washington State to cinch a Rose Bowl berth against Michigan.

Lettermen

Anthony Allen	John Gardenhire	Steve Pope
Tony Alvarado	Ken Gardner	William Reed
David Bayle	Scott Garnett	Mike Reilly
Ron Blacken	Danny Greene	Jim Rodgers
Andy Bresolin	Ken Hamer	Willie Rosborough
Dennis Brown	Derek Harvey	Phil Skansi
Tom Burnham	Ray Horton	Bill Stapleton
Tony Caldwell	Ron Jackson	Kyle Stevens
Rich Camarillo	Chris James	Mark Stewart
James Carter	Fletcher Jenkins	Brian Stone
Dario Casarino	Mark Jerue	Roger Tarver
Ray Cattage	Leroy Lutu	Scott Thompson
David Clawson	Curt Marsh	Toussaint Tyler
Paul Coty	Jerry McLain	Randy Van Divier
Tim Cowan	Eric Moran	Ron Wheeler
Mike Curtis	Chuck Nelson	Aaron Williams
Don Dow	Lance Neubauer	Greg Williams
Ken Driscoll	Vince Newsome	Darren Witcher
Scott Fausett	Chris O'Connor	Pat Zakskorn
Tom Flick	Rusty Olsen	John Zeger
Bret Gagliardi	Chris Pallis	

1981

Record: 10-2-0		Finish: PAC-10 lst		Coach: Don James	
Date	**UW**	**Opponent**			**Attendance**
Sept. 12	34	Pacific	14		45,134
Sept. 19	20	Kansas State	3		52,343
Sept. 26	17	at Oregon	3		40,695
Oct. 3	7	Arizona State	26		50,410
Oct. 10	27	at California	25		33,600
Oct. 17	56	Oregon State	17		52,324
Oct. 24	14	at Texas Tech	7		36,335
Oct. 31	42	Stanford	31		53,504
Nov. 7	0	at UCLA	31		41,818
Nov. 14	13	Southern Cal	3		59,870
Nov. 21	23	Washington St.	10		60,052
Jan. 1	28	Iowa (Rose Bowl)	0		105,611
Totals:	**281**		**171**		**631,696**

Co-Captains: James Carter, Vince Coby, Fletcher Jenkins, Mark Jerue.

Honors

Guy Flaherty: Vince Coby. **L. Walt Rising:** Fletcher Jenkins, James Carter. **Brian Stapp:** Pat Conrad. **Bob Jarvis:** Jim Holzknecht. **All-American:** Ray Horton. **All-Coast:** Fletcher Jenkins, Chuck Nelson, Mark Jerue.

Commentary

A solid team which would have finished in the top ten rankings if not for two very bad games; a 26-7 loss at Arizona State and a 31-0 shellacking at the hands of UCLA. The Bruins continue to be Washington's historical nemisis.

Lettermen

Vince Albritton	Scott Garnett	Chris O'Connor
Anthony Allen	Danny Greene	Ralph Parks
Tony Alvarado	Derek Harvey	Jeff Partridge
Cary Bailey	Stewart Hill	Steve Pelluer
Bob Brennan	Sterling Hinds	Jacque Robinson
Andy Bresolin	Ray Horton	Jim Rodgers
Ted Brose	Ron Jackson	Willie Rosborough
Dennis Brown	Chris James	Phil Skansi
Dean Browning	Fletcher Jenkins	Fred Small
Tony Caldwell	Mark Jerue	David Smith
James Carter	Joe Krakoski	Bill Stapleton
Ray Cattage	Robert Leaphart	Mark Stewart
Vince Coby	Leroy Lutu	Brian Stone
Michael Collins	Lynn Madsen	Scott Thompson
Pat Conrad	Dennis Maher	David Trimble
Paul Coty	Rick Mallory	Paul Van Hoosier
Tim Cowan	Bill Marshall	Doug Weston
Brenno DeFeo	David Matthews	David Whitenight
Lance Dodson	Tim Meamber	Aaron Williams
Don Dow	Jim Mora	Darren Witcher
Ken Driscoll	Eric Moran	Tony Wroten
Scott Fausset	Chuck Nelson	Pat Zakskorn
John Gardenhire	Vince Newsome	John Zeger

1982

Record: 10-2-0		Finish: PAC-10 2nd		Coach: Don James
Date	**UW**	**Opponent**		**Attendance**
Sept. 1	55	Texas El Paso (night)	0	55,649
Sept. 18	23	Arizona	13	48,984
Sept. 25	37	Oregon	21	58,742
Oct. 2	46	San Diego State	25	57,211
Oct. 9	50	California	7	58,522
Oct. 16	34	at Oregon State	17	38,000
Oct. 23	10	Texas Tech	3	59,318
Oct. 30	31	at Stanford	43	53,871
Nov. 6	10	UCLA	7	69,936
Nov. 13	17	at Arizona State	13	72,021
Nov. 20	20	at Washington St.	24	36,571
Dec. 25	21	Maryland (Aloha Bowl)	20	30,055
Totals:	**354**		**193**	**629,880**

Co-Captains: Anthony Allen, Ken Driscoll, Paul Skanski, Mark Stewart.

Honors

Guy Flaherty: Tom Cowan. **L. Walt Rising:** Eric Moran. **Brian Stapp:** Rick Dupree. **Bob Jarvis:** Mike Storey. **All-American:** Chuck Nelson, Tony Caldwell, Mark Stewart. **All-Coast:** Chuck Nelson, Mark Stewart, Jacque Robinson.

Commentary

One of the best Husky editions of the decade, ranked number one in both national polls for seven straight weeks before suffering a 43-31 loss at Stanford lead by quarterback John Elway. But the most stunning loss was the last game - 24-20 against arch rival Washington State at Pullman, the first time the Apple Cup had been played in Pullman since 1954.

Lettermen

Vince Albritton	Andy Fuimaono	Chris O'Connor
Anthony Allen	Scott Garnett	Jeff Partridge
Tony Alvarado	Stewart Hill	Mark Pattison
Ted Brose	Sterling Hinds	Steve Pelluer
Dennis Brown	Ron Holmes	Tim Peoples
Dean Browning	Ray Horton	Jacque Robinson
Tom Burnham	Chris James	Willie Rosborough
Tony Caldwell	Kevin Ikeda	Paul Skansi
Ray Cattage	Joe Kelly	Fred Small
Michael Collins	James Kirkpatrick	Tony Spearman
Pat Conrad	Joe Krakoski	Bill Stapleton
Paul Coty	Rob Kuharski	Mark Stewart
Tim Cowan	Robert Leaphart	Brian Stone
Doug Crow	Leroy Lutu	Mike Storey
Frank Cunningham	Lynn Madsen	David Stransky
Bill Daley	Rick Mallory	Scott Thompson
Sam Dancy	Tim Meamber	Paul Wagner
Lawrence Dodson	Larry Michael	Doug Weston
Phil Dormaier	Ron Milus	David Whitenight
Don Dow	Jim Mora	Aaron Williams
Ken Driscoll	Eric Moran	Darren Witcher
Dan Eernissee	Chuck Nelson	Tony Wroten
Scott Fausset	Vince Newsome	Pat Zakskorn

1983

Record: 8-4-0   **Finish:** PAC-10 2nd   **Coach:** Don James

Date	UW	Opponent		Attendance
Sept. 10	34	at Northwestern	0	26,165
Sept. 17	25	Michigan	24	60,638
Sept. 24	14	at Louisiana State	40	82,390
Oct. 1	27	Navy	7	59,912
Oct. 8	34	Oregon State	7	60,354
Oct. 15	32	Stanford	15	60,270
Oct. 22	32	at Oregon	3	44,303
Oct. 29	24	at UCLA	27	60,094
Nov. 5	23	at Arizona	22	48,808
Nov. 12	24	Southern Cal	0	60,690
Nov. 19	6	Washington State	17	59,220
Dec. 25	10	Penn State (Aloha Bowl)	13	37,212
Totals:	**285**		**178**	**666,056**

Co-Captains: Stewart Hill, Dave Browning, Rick Mallory, Steve Pelluer.

Honors

Guy Flaherty: Steve Pelluer. **L. Walt Rising:** Rick Mallory, Ron Homes. **Brian Stapp:** Hugh Millen. **Bob Jarvis:** Jeff Wilmoth. **All-Coast:** Steve Pelluer, Rick Mallory.

Commentary

Once again, one game kept the Huskies out of Pasadena, this time a loss at UCLA, their historic nemesis, 27-24. In this game future Husky coach Rick Neuheisel completed a NCAA record 25 of 27 passes. That resulted in the Huskies being detoured to Honolulu for an Aloha Bowl match with Penn State.

Lettermen

Dan Agen
Vince Albritton
John Allen
Tony Alvarado
Kenny Baldwin
Ted Brose
Dean Browning
Blaise Chappell
Thane Cleland
Michael Collins
Doug Crow
Brenno DeFeo
Lance Dodson
Tony Dominique
Dan Eernissee
Rick Fenney
Scott Garnett
Danny Greene
Ron Hadley
Lonzell Hill
Stewart Hill
Sterling Hinds
Ron Holmes
Walt Hunt
Ron Jackson
Vestee Jackson
Jeff Jaeger
Allen James
Joe Kelly
Stewart Keyes
James Kirkpatrick
Joe Krakoski
Rob Kuharski
Robert Leaphart
Tony Lewis
Leroy Luto
Lynn Madsen
Dennis Maher
Rick Mallory
Tim Meamber
Larry Michael
Ron Milus
Jim Mora
Mark Pattison
J.C. Pearson
Steve Pelluer
Al Robertson
Jacque Robinson
Jim Rodgers
John Skanski
Fred Small
Shannon Smith
Dennis Soldat
David Stransky
Roger Tarver
David Trimble
Albert Tufono
Lacy Walker
David Whitenght
Darren Wilson
Tony Wroten

1984

Record: 11-1-0 **Finish:** PAC-10 2nd **Coach:** Don James

Date	UW	Opponent		Attendance
Sept. 8	26	Northwestern	0	55,364
Sept. 15	20	at Michigan	11	103,072
Sept. 22	35	Houston	7	61,045
Oct. 29	53	Miami (Ohio)	7	56,900
Oct. 6	19	at Oregon State	7	40,000
Oct. 13	37	at Stanford	15	44,500
Oct. 20	17	Oregon	10	58,088
Oct. 27	28	Arizona	12	59,876
Nov. 3	44	California	14	59,462
Nov. 10	7	at Southern Cal	16	71,838
Nov. 17	38	at Washington State	29	40,000
Jan. 1	28	Oklahoma (Orange Bowl)	17	56,294
Totals:	**352**		**145**	**706,439**

Co-Captains: Dan Eernissee, Danny Greene, Tim Meamber, Jim Rodgers.

Honors

Guy Flaherty: Jim Rodgers. **L. Walt Rising:** Ron Holmes. **Brian Stapp:** Eric Dahlquist. **Bob Jarvis:** Donnie Morehead. **All-American:** Ron Holmes. **All-Coast:** Ron Holmes, Tim Meamber, Jim Rodgers.

Commentary

One more time, one late season loss, detoured the Huskies from Pasadena. And once again the scene of the accident was Los Angeles, a 17-6 loss to Southern Cal. The detour sent Washington to the Orange Bowl and a meeting with Oklahoma. The 1984 edition of Huskies is still considered one of the greatest Washington defensive teams of all time.

Lettermen

Dan Agen	Ron Holmes	Tim Peoples
John Allen	Walt Hunt	David Rill
Steve Alvord	Jeff Jaeger	Jay Roberts
Rich Barber	Cookie Jackson	Al Robertson
Garland Beardon	Vestee Jackson	Jacque Robinson
Dwight Bibbs	Allen James	Jim Rodgers
Tim Burnham	Rod Jones	Reggie Rodgers
Steve Busz	Joe Kelly	Sauni Savini
Chris Chandler	James Kirkpatrick	Paul Sicuro
Thane Cleland	Joe Krakoski	Fred Small
Doug Crow	Bruce Kroon	Brett Smith
Eric Dahlquist	Rob Kuharski	Dennis Soldat
Brenno DeFeo	Eric Lambright	Garth Thomas
Dan Eernissee	Mark Larsen	David Toy
Lance Fauria	Tony Lewis	David Trimble
Rick Fenney	Dennis Maher	Albert Tufono
Darryl Franklin	Tim Meamber	Paul Waskom
Mike Gaffney	Hugh Millen	Jeff Wilmoth
Kevin Gogan	Ron Milus	Tony Wroten
Danny Greene	Donnie Morehead	Bo Yates
Ron Hadley	Mark Pattison	
Lonzell Hill	J.C. Pearson	

1985

Record: 7-5-0		Finish: PAC-10 4th		Coach: Don James
Date	**UW**	**Opponent**		**Attendance**
Sept. 7	17	Oklahoma State	31	60,320
Sept. 14	3	at Brigham Young	31	65,476
Sept. 21	29	at Houston	12	20,522
Sept. 28	21	UCLA	14	60,425
Oct. 5	19	at Oregon	13	44,383
Oct. 12	28	at California	12	49,000
Oct. 19	20	Oregon State	21	58,771
Nov. 2	34	Stanford	0	58,625
Nov. 9	7	at Arizona State	36	67,474
Nov. 16	20	Southern Cal	17	59,417
Nov. 23	20	Washington State	21	59,887
Dec. 30	20	Colorado (Freedom Bowl)	17	30,961
Totals:	**238**		**225**	**635,261**

Co-Captains: Joe Kelly, Vestee Jackson, Hugh Millen, Dennis Soldat.

Honors

Guy Flaherty: Joe Kelley. **L. Walt Rising:** Dan Agen. **Brian Stapp:** Sean Bergman. **Bob Jarvis:** Joe Bracken. **All-Coast:** Joe Kelley, Reggie Rogers.

Commentary

Many of the key players from the 1984 team moved on, many to the NFL and this edition was a rebuilding year. The low point of the season was a home loss to Oregon State 21-20; the Huskies entered the game a 37-point favorite. Every Beaver has to have his day. They say.

Lettermen

Dan Agen	Kevin Gogan	Tim Peoples
Steve Alvord	Ron Hadley	David Rill
Ricky Andrews	Andre Hayes	Steve Roberts
Bruce Beall	Lonzell Hill	Reggie Rogers
Flip Brown	Steve Holzgraf	Brian Slater
Tim Burnham	Vestee Jackson	Brett Smith
Steve Busz	Jeff Jaeger	Dennis Soldat
Chris Chandler	Allen James	Garth Thomas
John Chapman	Aaron Jenkins	David Trimble
Blaise Chappell	Rod Jones	David Walker
Thane Cleland	Scott Jones	Bob Waskom
Tony Covington	Joe Kelly	Paul Waskom
Tony Dominique	Eric Lambright	Vince Weathersby
Tom Erlandson	Mark Larsen	Brett Wiese
Rick Fenney	Art Malone	Demouy Williams
Scott Fitzgerald	Jim Matthews	Bob Willig
Darryl Franklin	Keilan Matthews	Bo Yates
Vince Fudzie	Rick Meyer	Tony Zackery
Andy Fuimaono	Hugh Millen	Mike Zandofsky
Mike Gafney	Ron Milus	

1986

Record: 8-3-1		Finish: PAC-10 Tie 2nd		Coach: Don James
Date	UW	Opponent		Attendance
Sept. 13	40	Ohio State	7	60,071
Sept. 20	52	Brigham Young	21	61,197
Sept. 27	10	at Southern Cal	20	58,023
Oct. 4	50	California	18	58,911
Oct. 11	24	at Stanford	14	52,000
Oct. 18	48	Bowling Green	0	57,075
Oct. 25	38	Oregon	3	58,466
Nov. 1	21	at Arizona State (night)	34	71,589
Nov. 8	28	at Oregon State	12	29,541
Nov. 15	17	UCLA	17	59,916
Nov. 22	44	at Washington State	23	40,000
Dec. 25	6	Alabama (Sun Bowl)	28	48,722
Totals:	378		197	655,511

Co-Captains: Steve Alvord, Kevin Gogan, Rick Fenney, Rod Jones, Tim Peoples, Reggie Rogers.

Honors

Guy Flaherty: Steve Alvord. **L. Walt Rising:** Reggie Rogers. **Brian Stapp:** Jim Ferrell. **Bob Jarvis:** Todd Kester. **All-America:** Jeff Jaeger. **All-Coast:** Rick Fenney, Lonzell Hill, Jeff Jaeger, Tim Peoples, Reggie Rogers.

Commentary

This was a team despite its spectacular beginning fizzled to a lackluster ending. At the Sun Bowl in El Paso against Alabama the team looked so tired and slow in the second half that there was speculation they had spent the night before across the border in Jaurez quaffing Tequila, the band's trademark theme song.

Lettermen

Steve Alvord
Bill Ames
Ricky Andrews
Bruce Beall
Joseph Bracken
Bern Brostek
Dennis Brown
Steve Busz
Chris Chandler
Thane Cleland
David Cole
Tony Covington
Tom Erlandson
Rick Fenney
Darryl Franklin
Mike Gaffney
Kevin Gogan
Clay Griffith
Brian Habib
Darryl Hall
Martin Harrison

David Hawkins
Lonzell Hill
Steve Holzgraf
Gary Hyatt
Jeff Jaeger
Allen James
Aaron Jenkins
Scott Jones
Steve Jones
Le-Lo Lang
Mark Larsen
Frank Lutu
Art Malone
Keilan Matthews
Mike Matz
Rick McLeod
Ricky Meyer
James Mitchell
Joel Navarro
Tim Peoples
Will Rideout

Andre Riley
David Rill
Jay Roberts
Steve Roberts
Reggie Rogers
James Simpson
Brian Slater
George Smith
Garth Thomas
David Toy
Greg Travis
Paul Waskom
Vince Weathersby
Brett Wiese
Demouy Williams
Bob Willig
Bo Yates
Tony Zackery
Mike Zandofsky

1987

Record: 7-4-1		Finish: PAC-10 3rd		Coach: Don James
Date	UW	Opponent		Attendance
Sept. 5	31	Stanford	21	73,676
Sept. 12	28	Purdue	10	70,492
Sept. 19	12	at Texas A & M	29	58,178
Sept. 26	31	Pacific	3	69,605
Oct. 3	22	at Oregon	29	44,421
Oct. 10	27	Arizona State	14	73,883
Oct. 17	23	Southern Cal	37	71,678
Oct. 31	28	Oregon State	12	66,392
Nov. 7	21	at Arizona	21	50,021
Nov. 14	14	at UCLA	47	70,332
Nov. 21	34	Washington State	19	74,038
Dec. 19	24	Tulane (Independence Bowl)	12	41,693
Totals:	295		254	764,409

Co-Captains: Chris Chandler, Darryl Franklin, Brian Habib, David Rill.

Honors

Guy Flaherty: Darryl Franklin. **L. Walt Rising:** Brian Habib. **Brian Stapp:** Thomas Pearson. **Bob Jarvis:** Mark West. **All-America:** Mike Zandofsky. **All-Coast:** Mike Zandofsky.

Commentary

The new upper deck on the north side of the stadium was dedicated with the 31-21 victory over Stanford, but it was about the only thing to celebrate in 1987. Unless one counts the victory over Tulane at the Independence Bowl. The what?

Lettermen

Mike Allman
Bill Ames
Johnny Anderson
Ricky Andrews
Bruce Beall
Curtis Bell
Eric Briscoe
Bern Brostek
Dennis Brown
Brandee Brownlee
Eugene Burkhalter
Chris Chandler
Jeff Chandler
Chris Cheeks
James Compton
Cary Conklin
Adam Cooney
Tony Covington
Mark DeGross
Pat Doyle
Tom Erlandson
Tim Esary
Scott Fitzgerald
Darryl Franklin
Brian Habib
Darryl Hall
Martin Harrison
David Hawkins
Art Hunter
Aaron Jenkins
Kelly John-Lewis
Mark Jones
Scott Jones
Steve Jones
Dan Kahn
Todd Kester
Mark Kilpack
Jeff Kohlwes
Le-Lo Lang
Greg Lewis
Shawn Lightning
Brent Locknane
Frank Lutu
Art Malone
Mike Matz
Rick McLeod
Ricky Meyer
Jeff Pahukoa
Doug Parry
Doug Petrich
Mark Poole
Travis Richarson
Will Rideout
Andre Riley
David Rill
Mitch Robbins
Jay Roberts
Brian Slater
Tarn Sublett
David Toy
Greg Travis
Albert Tufono
Jim Waskom
Vince Weathersby
Brett Wiese
Demouy Williams
Bob Willig
Bo Yates
Tony Zackery
Mike Zandofsky

1988

Record: 6-5-0		Finish: PAC-10 6th		Coach: Don James
Date	UW	Opponent		Attendance
Sept. 10	20	at Purdue	6	56,126
Sept. 17	31	Army	17	66,128
Sept. 24	35	San Jose State	31	63,692
Oct. 1	17	UCLA	24	71,224
Oct. 8	10	at Arizona State	0	70,934
Oct. 15	27	at Southern Cal	28	62,974
Oct. 22	14	at Oregon	17	45,978
Oct. 29	28	Stanford	25	68,272
Nov. 5	13	Arizona	16	65,604
Nov. 12	28	California	27	58,823
Nov. 19	31	at Washington State	32	40,000
Totals:	254		223	669,755

Co-Captains: Ricky Andrews, Darryl Hall, Aaron Jenkins, Mike Zandofsky.

Honors
Guy Flaherty: Jim Ferrell. **L. Walt Rising:** Bern Brostek. **Brian Stapp:** Marc West. **Bob Jarvis:** Jim Ferrell. **All-Coast:** Dennis Brown.

Commentary
This edition lost five games by a total of 15 points which lead to *The Winter of Our Discontent* and Don James decision to infuse new blood into the Husky brain trust. Enter Dennis Gilberston to rescue a stagnating program which did not get invited to a bowl game for the first time in nine seasons.

Lettermen

Mike Allman	Marc Goudeau	Darren McKinney
Bill Ames	Dana Hall	Andy Munro
Eric Briscoe	Darryl Hall	Dorie Murray
Bern Brostek	Martin Harrison	Jeff Pahukoa
Dennis Brown	David Hawkins	Dorie Murray
Eugene Burkhalter	Art Hunter	Aaron Pierce
Eric Canton	Aaron Jenkins	Mark Poole
Jeff Chandler	Kelly John-Lewis	Ivory Randle
James Clifford	Donald Jones	Travis Richardson
Brett Collins	Mark Jones	Andre Riley
James Compton	Scott Jones	Roland Ruff
Cary Conklin	Steve Jones	James Sawyer
Adam Cooney	Virgil Jones	Brian Slater
Tony Covington	Mark Kilpack	George Smith
Ed Cunningham	Dean Kirkland	Greg Travis
Michael Darden	Jeff Kohlwes	Jim Waskom
Mark DeGross	Le-Lo Lang	Keith Watkins
William Doctor	Greg Lewis	Vince Weathersby
Chris Downes	Garrett Lordahl	Brett Wiese
Pat Doyle	Siupeli Malamala	Bob Willig
Jim Ferrell	Art Malone	Tony Zackery
Scott Fitzgerald	Mike Matz	Mike Zandofsky
Chico Fraley	John McCallum	

1989

Record: 8-4-0		Finish: PAC-10 2nd		Coach: Don James
Date	UW	Opponent		Attendance
Sept. 9	19	Texas A & M	6	69,434
Sept. 16	38	Purdue	9	66,392
Sept. 23	17	at Arizona	20	50,935
Sept. 30	28	Colorado	45	69,152
Oct. 7	16	at Southern Cal	24	58,410
Oct. 14	20	Oregon	14	70,442
Oct. 21	29	at California	16	20,000
Oct. 28	28	at UCLA	27	48,801
Nov. 4	32	Arizona State	34	64,695
Nov. 11	51	at Oregon State	14	32,147
Nov. 18	20	Washington State	9	73,527
Dec. 30	34	Florida (Freedom Bowl)	7	33,858
Totals:	332		225	657,793

Co-Captains: Dennis Brown, Cary Conklin, Martin Harrison, Andre Riley.

Honors

Guy Flaherty: Andre Riley. **L. Walt Rising:** Martin Harrison, **Brian Stapp:** Matt Jones. **Bob Jarvis:** Mark DeGross. **All-Coast:** Dennis Brown.

Commentary

From *The Winter Of Our Discontent* came a season where *The Sun Also Rises.* If one looked closely they could see the genesis of a national champion taking root: Steve Emtman, Mario Bailey, Beno Bryant, Donald Jones, Aaron Pierce, Dana Hall, Lincoln Kennedy, and waiting in the wings an unknown left handed quarterback, Mark Brunnel. All the pieces were there - waiting.

Lettermen

Mike Allman	Steve Emtman	Mike Lustyk
Eric Alozie	Jaime Fields	Siupeli Malamala
Bill Ames	Chico Fraley	Caesar Malvar
Mario Bailey	Marc Goudeau	Mike Matz
Jay Barry	Dana Hall	John McCallum
Eric Briscoe	Martin Harrison	Orlando McKay
Bern Brostek	Harold Hasselbach	Tony McNair
Corey Brown	Rick Hicks	Charles Mincy
Dennis Brown	Dave Hoffman	Jeff Pahukoa
Beno Bryant	Art Hunter	Shane Pahukoa
Eugene Burkhalter	Todd Jerome	Aaron Pierce
Eric Canton	Chris Jolley	Travis Richardson
Jeff Chandler	Donald Jones	Andre Riley
James Clifford	Marc Jones	Rick Schulberg
Brett Collins	Mark Jones	Tommie Smith
James Compton	Virgil Jones	Greg Travis
Cary Conklin	Lincoln Kennedy	Darius Turner
John Cook	Mark Kilpack	Marc West
Adam Cooney	Dean Kirkland	Alan Weyrick
Ed Cunningham	Jeff Kohlwes	Channing Wyles
Mark DeGross	Le-Lo Lang	
William Doctor	Greg Lewis	

1990

Record: 10-2-0		**Finish:** PAC-10 lst		**Coach:** Don James	
Date	**UW**	**Opponent**			**Attendance**
Sept. 8	20	San Jose State		17	66,337
Sept. 15	20	at Purdue		14	33,113
Sept. 22	31	Southern California		0	72,617
Sept. 29	14	at Colordao		20	52,868
Oct. 6	42	at Arizona State		14	62,738
Oct. 13	38	Oregon		17	73,498
Oct. 20	52	at Stanford		16	36,600
Oct. 27	46	California		7	71,427
Nov. 3	54	Arizona		10	70,111
Nov. 10	22	UCLA		25	71,925
Nov. 17	55	at Washington State		10	37,600
Jan. 1	46	Iowa (Rose Bowl)		34	101,273
Totals:	**394**			**150**	**750,107**

Co-Captains: Eric Briscoe, Dean Kirkland, Greg Lewis, Travis Richardson.

Honors

Guy Flaherty: Greg Lewis. **L. Walt Rising:** Steve Emtman. **Brian Stapp:** Jeff Aselin. **Bob Jarvis:** Jay Wells. **All-American:** Greg Lewis. **All-Conference:** Beno Bryant, Steve Emtman, Donald Jones, Dean Kirkland, Greg Lewis, Charles Mincy, Jeff Pahukoa, Travis Richardson.

Commentary

If anyone was watching carefully, this was a work of art in progress which blossmed the next year into a season of perfection.

Lettermen

Mario Bailey	Jaime Fields	Mike Lustyk
Walter Bailey	Jamal Fountaine	Siupeli Malamala
Jay Barry	Chico Fraley	Andy Mason
Eric Briscoe	Curtis Gaspard	Orlando McKay
Mark Brunnell	Dana Hall	Charles Mincy
Beno Bryant	Travis Hanson	Lamar Mitchell
Hillary Butler	Richard Hicks	Jeff Pahukoa
Brent Collins	Dave Hoffman	Shane Pahukoa
John Cook	Jason Jensen	Aaron Pierce
Adam Cooney	Leif Johnson	Travis Richardson
Ed Cunningham	Donald Jones	Tyronne Rodgers
Mark DeGross	Matt Jones	Rich Schulberg
William Doctor	Virgil Jones	Danianke Smith
Mike Dodd	Lincoln Kennedy	Steve Springstead
Mark DeGross	Dean Kirkland	Darius Turner
P.A. Emerson	Joe Kralik	Channing Wyles
Steve Emtman	Greg Lewis	

1991

Record: 12-0-0		Finish: PAC-10 lst		Coach: Don James
Date	**UW**	**Opponent**		**Attendance**
Sept. 7	42	at Stanford	7	45,273
Sept. 21	36	at Nebrasksa	21	76,304
Sept. 28	56	Kansas State	3	71,638
Oct. 5	54	Arizona	0	72,495
Oct. 12	48	Toledo	0	72,738
Oct. 19	24	at California	17	74,500
Oct. 26	29	Oregon	7	72,318
Nov. 2	44	Arizona State	16	72,405
Nov. 9	14	at Southern California	3	59,320
Nov. 16	58	at Oregon State	6	31,588
Nov. 23	56	Washington State	21	72,581
Jan. 1	34	Michigan (Rose Bowl)	14	103,566
Totals:	**461**		**101**	**824,254**

Co-Captains: Mario Bailey, Brett Collins, Ed Cunningham, Donald Jones,

Honors

Guy Flaherty: Mark Brunnell. **L. Walt Rising:** Lincoln Kennedy. **Brian Stapp:** Mark Schilder. **Bob Jarvis:** Tom Nakene. **All-American:** Mario Bailey, Steve Emtman, Dave Hoffmann. **All-Conference:** Mario Bailey, Ed Cunningham, Steve Emtman, Chico Fraley, Dana Hall, Dave Hoffmann, Donald Jones.

Commentary

Every college football team should have just one season like this one: *perfection*. If there ever was a perfect college football team this one was it. Perfect balance: there was no weakness in this team. Some argue it was the best college team ever. (See chapter 18 for a review of the team and season.)

Lettermen

Bruce Bailey	Jamal Fountaine	Andy Mason
Mario Bailey	Chico Fraley	Shell Mays
Walter Bailey	Tom Gallagher	Orlando McKay
Damon Barry	Curtis Gaspard	Josh Moore
Jay Barry	Frank Garcia	Jim Nevelle
Eric Bjornson	Dana Hall	Shane Pahukoa
Mark Brunnell	Travis Hanson	Andrew Peterson
Mark Breuner	Billy Joe Hobart	Aaron Pierce
Beno Bryant	Dave Hoffman	Pete Pierson
Hillary Butler	Leif Johnson	Dan Posey
Richie Chambers	Donald Jones	Dante Robinson
James Clifford	Louis Jones	Tyronne Rodgers
Brett Collins	Matt Jones	Kris Rongen
Jason Crabbe	Pete Kaligis	Donovan Schmidt
Ed Cunningham	Napoleon Kaufman	Danianke Smith
Mike Derrow	Lincoln Kennedy	Tommie Smith
William Doctor	David Killpatrick	Steve Springstead
Steve Emtman	Joe Kralik	Scott Stuart
D'Marco Farr	Lamar Lyons	Darius Turner
Jaime Fields	Damon Mack	John Werdel

1992

Record: 9-3-0		Finish: PAC-10 1st		Coach: Don James
Date	UW	Opponent		Attendance
Sept. 5	31	at Arizona State	7	53,782
Sept. 12	27	Wisconsin	10	72,800
Sept. 19	29	Nebraska (night)	14	73,333
Oct. 3	17	Southern California	10	73,275
Oct. 10	35	California	16	73,504
Oct. 17	24	at Oregon	3	47,612
Oct. 24	31	Pacific	7	70,618
Oct. 31	41	Stanford	7	70,821
Nov. 7	3	at Arizona (night)	16	58,510
Nov. 14	45	Oregon State	16	70,419
Nov. 21	23	at Washington State	42	37,600
Jan. 1	31	Michigan (Rose Bowl)	38	94,236
Totals:	306		148	794,510

Co-Captains: Mark Brunell, Dave Hoffman, Lincoln Kennedy, Shane Pahukoa.

Honors

Guy Flaherty: Dave Hoffmann. L. Walt Rising: Lincoln Kennedy. Brian Stapp: Ikaika Malloe. Bob Jarvis: John Fiala. All-American: Dave Hoffmann, Lincoln Kennedy. All-Conference: Dave Hoffmann, Napoleon Kaufman, Lincoln Kennedy.

Commentary

This team managed to return to the Rose Bowl for the third consecutive time, but it did so limping, losing two of its final three games. And it fell under a cloud of scandal as starting quarterback Billy Joe Hobart was found to have accepted illegal loans that was to bring about the final season for Coach Don James. (See chapter 7.)

Lettermen

Bruce Bailey
Walter Bailey
Damon Barry
Jay Barry
Eric Bjornson
Mark Breuner
Todd Bridge
Mark Brunnell
Hillery Butler
Richie Chambers
James Clifford
Ernie Conwell
D'Marco Farr
Jaime Fields
Jamal Fountaine
Tom Gallagher
Frank Garcia

Phil Green
Travis Hanson
Russell Hairiston
Eugene Harris
Dave Hoffman
Steve Hoffman
Leif Johnson
Louis Jones
Matt Jones
Napoleon Kaufman
Lincoln Kennedy
Patrick Kesi
David Killpatrick
Joe Kralik
Mike Lustyk
Lamar Lyons
Andy Mason

Josh Moore
Shaun Moore
Tom Nakane
Jim Nevelle
Shane Pahukoa
Andrew Peterson
Pete Pierson
Dante Robinson
Donovan Schmidt
Jason Shelley
Tommie Smith
Steve Springstead
Justin Thomas
Richard Thomas
Darius Turner
John Werdel

1993

Record: 7-4-0		Finish: PAC-10 4th		Coach: Jim Lambright
Date	**UW**	**Opponent**		**Attendance**
Sept. 4	31	Stanford	14	71,893
Sept. 11	12	at Ohio State	21	94,109
Sept. 25	35	East Carolina	0	72,108
Oct. 2	52	San Jose State	17	67,976
Oct. 9	24	at California	23	55,000
Oct. 16	25	at UCLA	39	40,830
Oct. 23	21	Oregon	6	72,534
Oct. 30	17	at Arizona State	32	48,116
Nov. 6	28	at Oregon State	21	33,944
Nov. 13	17	Southern California	22	72,202
Nov. 20	26	Washington State	3	72,688
Totals:	**288**		**198**	**701,400**

Co-Captains: Jamal Fountaine, Matt Jones, Andy Mason, Jim Nevelle.

Honors

Guy Flaherty: Pete Kaligis. **L. Walt Rising:** Pete Pierson. **Brian Stapp:** Jason Chorak. **Bob Jarvis:** Ikaika Malloe. **All-American:** Mark Breuner. **All-Conference:** Mark Breuner, Tom Gallagher, Napoleon Kaufman.

Commentary

Washington was placed on two years probation by the PAC-10 Commissioners and prohibited from participating in any post season bowl competition. In protest of these penalties Coach Don James resigned on August 23rd. Defensive Coach Jim Lambright was named his successor.

Lettermen

Damon Barry	Frank Garcia	Andy Mason
Eric Bjornson	Russell Hairston	D.J. McCarthy
Mark Breuner	Trevor Highfield	Lawyer Milloy
Hillery Butler	Damon Huard	Jim Nevelle
Beno Bryant	Dave Janoski	Shane Pahukoa
Richie Chambers	Jerry Jenson	Andrew Peterson
Ernie Conwell	Leif Johnson	Pete Pierson
Jason Crabbe	Louis Jones	David Ritchie
Deke Devers	Matt Jones	Donovan Schmidt
P.A. Emerson	Napoleon Kaufman	Steve Springstead
Mike Ewaliko	Patrick Kesi	Justin Thomas
D'Marco Farr	David Killpatrick	Richard Thomas
John Fiala	Joe Kralik	John Werdel
Jamal Fountaine	Lamar Lyons	Cedric White
Tom Gallagher	Ikaika Malloe	Don Willis

1994

Record: 7-4-0		Finish: PAC-10 tie 4th		Coach: Jim Lambright
Date	UW	Opponent		Attendance
Sept. 3	17	at Southern California	24	54,538
Sept. 10	25	Ohio State	16	70,861
Sept. 24	38	at Miami (Fla.)	20	62,663
Oct. 1	37	UCLA	10	71,851
Oct. 8	34	San Jose State	20	69,448
Oct. 15	35	Arizona State	14	69,335
Oct. 22	20	at Oregon	31	44,134
Oct. 29	24	Oregon State	10	70,071
Nov. 5	28	at Stanford (night)	46	44,200
Nov. 12	31	California	19	69,618
Nov. 19	6	at Washington State	23	37,600
Totals:	295		233	664,319

Co-Captains: David Killpatrick, Donovan Schmidt, Mark Bruener, Napoleon Kaufman.

Honors

Guy Flaherty: Richard Thomas. **L. Walt Rising:** Fank Garcia. **Brian Stapp:** Josh Smith. **Bob Jarvis:** Stuart Williams. **All-Conference:** Mark Breuner, Frank Garcia, Napoleon Kaufman, Lawyer Milloy.

Commentary

This was a team which had several great games and several bombs: there was the *whammy in Miami* and the *great give away* in Eugene - neither have been forgotten by friend or foes.

Lettermen

Ink Aleaga
Jeff Aselin
Eric Battle
Brooks Beaupain
Dwight Bibbs
Eric Bjornson
Mark Breuner
Chris Campbell
Richie Chambers
Jason Chorak
Cameron Cleeland
Fred Coleman
Ernie Conwell
Deke Devers
Rob Dibble
Mike Ewaliko
John Fiala
Shane Fortney
Frank Garcia
Russell Hairiston
Trevor Highfield
Steve Hoffman
Terry Holliman
Damon Huard
Dave Janoski
Jerry Jenson
Leif Johnson
Lynn Johnson
Louis Jones
Ryan Kadletz
Napoleon Kaufman
Patrick Kesi
David Killpatrick
Cam Kissel
Lamar Lyons
Ikaika Malloe
Lawyer Milloy
Tony Parrish
Andrew Peterson
Geoff Prince
Greg Quesada
Mike Reed
David Ritchie
Bob Sapp
Donovan Schmidt
Rashaan Shehee
Geoff Tamble
Justin Thomas
Richard Thomas
John Wales

1995

Record: 7-4-1		Finish: PAC-10 tied Ist		Coach: Jim Lambright
Date	**UW**	**Opponent**		**Attendance**
Sept. 2	23	Arizona State	20	73,129
Sept. 16	20	at Ohio State	30	94,104
Sept. 23	21	Army	13	*76,125
Sept. 30	26	at Oregon State	16	32,989
Oct. 7	21	Notre Dame	29	74,023
Oct. 14	38	at Stanford	28	45,210
Oct. 21	31	at Arizona	17	58,471
Oct. 28	21	Southern Cal	21	74,421
Nov. 4	22	Oregon	24	74,054
Nov. 11	38	at UCLA	14	50,104
Nov. 18	33	Washington State	30	74,144
Dec. 29	18	Iowa (Sun Bowl)	38	49,116
Totals:	**312**		**280**	**775,232**

Co-Captains: Ernie Conwell, Deke Devers, Stephen Hoffman, Richard Thomas. *Largest crowd in Husky Stadium history.

Honors

Guy Flaherty: Leon Neal. **L. Walt Rising:** Trevor Highfield. **Brian Stapp:** Arnie Maish. **Bob Jarvis:**Jeff Shoe. **All-American:**Lawyer Milloy. **All-Conference:** Ink Aleaga, Ernie Conwell, Lawyer Malloy.

Commentary

After 46 years the Notre Dame game is revived and the results are the same as 1949; a loss. But this game brings about *deja vu* in another way: *the great give away* in Eugene from 94'. The Huskies were in position to cinch a Rose Bowl invite if they defeat Southern Cal. But after leading 21-0 at the half, they allow the Trojans to score 21 unanswered second half points and SC goes to Pasadena. Another Husky detour to El Paso and a tequila *deja vu*.

Lettermen

Ink Aleaga	Matt Hicks	Aaron Nettles
Eric Battle	Trevor Highfield	Tony Parrish
Brooks Beaupain	Steve Hoffman	Jerome Pathon
Jesse Binkley	Terry Holliman	Geoff Prince
Jeremey Brigham	Damon Huard	Greg Quesada
Chris Campbell	Dave Janoski	Bob Sapp
Jason Chorak	Jerry Jenson	Eric Schlepp
Cameron Cleeland	Darius Jones	Opu Seminavage
Fred Coleman	Ryan Kadletz	Rashaan Shehee
Ernie Conwell	George Keiaho	Jeff Shoe
Aaron Dalan	Patrick Kesi	Josh Smith
Andre DeSaussure	Cam Kissel	Mostafa Sobbi
Deke Devers	Olin Kreutz	Richard Thomas
Mike Ewaliko	Alex Lacson	John Wales
John Fiala	Chris Lang	Sekou Wiggs
Shane Fortney	Ikaika Malloe	Chad Wolfe
Marques Hairston	Lawyer Milloy	
Andre Hays	Steve Morrison	

1996

Date	UW	Opponent		Attendance
Record: 9-3-0		Finish: PAC-10 2nd	Coach: Jim Lambright	
Sept. 7	42	at Arizona State (night)	45	73,379
Sept. 14	29	Brigham Young	17	71,165
Sept. 21	31	Arizona	17	73,414
Oct. 5	27	Stanford	6	71,488
Oct. 12	16	at Notre Dame	54	59,075
Oct. 19	41	UCLA	21	70,444
Oct. 26	33	at Oregon	14	46,226
Nov. 2	21	at Southern Cal	10	60 039
Nov. 9	42	Oregon State	3	71,072
Nov. 16	53	San Jose State	10	70,063
Nov. 23	31	at Washington State (ot)	24	37,600
Dec. 30	21	Colorado (Holiday Bowl)	33	54,749
Totals:	391		254	758,714

Co-Captains: Ink Aleaga, John Fiala, Bob Sapp, Dave Janoski.

Honors

Guy Flaherty: John Fiala. L. Walt Rising: Jason Chorak. Brian Stapp: Chris Waddell. Bob Jarvis: Ryan Miletich. All-American: Jason Chorak, Benji Olson. All-Conference: Ink Aleaga, Jason Chorak, Corey Dillon, Olin Kreutz, Benji Olson, Tony Parrish.

Commentary

Damon Huard graduates, much to the disappointment of Oregon fans, and his brother Brock takes his place. But the real story of 1996 is a new Husky addition, running back Corey Dillon. Although Dillon doesn't start until the third game of the year, he breaks records and is the most devastating Husky runner ever. Unfortunately after only one season Dillon moves on to the NFL, much to the relief of every other team in the conference.

Lettermen

Ink Aleaga	Jason Harris	Tony Parrish
Brooks Beaupain	Anthony Hicks	Jerome Pathon
Jesse Binkley	Chris Hoffman	Geoff Prince
Jeremy Brigham	Alex Hollowell	Mike Reed
Eddie Burrell	Brock Huard	David Ritchie
Nigel Burton	Dave Janoski	Bob Sapp
Chris Campbell	Joe Jarzynka	Hamid Sarshar
Jason Chorak	Jerry Jenson	Gary Shavey
Cameron Cleeland	Todd Johnson	Maurice Shaw
Tony Coats	Bredon Jones	Rashaan Shehee
Fred Coleman	Ben Kadletz	Jermaine Smith
Aaron Dalan	George Keiaho	Josh Smith
Dominic Daste	Petroceli Kesi	Mostafa Sobbi
Dave Dawson	Cam Kissel	Lester Towns
Corey Dillon	Olin Kreutz	Mac Tuiaea
John Fiala	Ikaika Malloe	John Wales
Shane Fortney	Mel Miller	Sekou Wiggs
Marques Hairston	Anthony Mizen	
Gerald Harris	Benji Olson	

1997

Record: 8-4-0		**Finish:** PAC-10 4th		**Coach:** Jim Lambright
Date	**UW**	**Opponent**		**Attendance**
Sept. 6	42	at Brigham Young	20	65,978
Sept. 13	36	San Diego State	3	71,081
Sept. 20	14	Nebraska	27	74,023
Oct. 4	26	Arizona State	14	74,986
Oct. 11	30	at California	3	48,000
Oct. 18	58	at Arizona	28	50,585
Oct. 25	45	at Oregon State	17	28,067
Nov. 1	27	Southern Cal	0	73 104
Nov. 8	28	Oregon	31	73,775
Nov. 15	28	at UCLA	52	85,697
Nov. 22	35	Washington State	41	74,268
Dec. 25	51	Michigan St. (Aloha Bowl)	23	34,419
Totals:	**420**		**259**	**754,280**

Co-Captains: Jerry Jensen, Rashaan Shehee, Jerome Pathon, Tony Parrish.

Honors

Guy Flaherty: Olin Kreutz. **L. Walt Rising:** Olin Kreutz. **Brian Stapp:** Andy Nevens. **Bob Jarvis:** Gary Shavey. **All-American:** Olin Kreutz, Benji Olson, Jerome Pathon. **All-Conference:** Jason Chorak, Cam Cleeland, Jerry Jensen, Olin Kreutz, Benji Olson, Jerome Pathon, Rashaan Shehee.

Commentary

Injuries late in the season to quarterback Brock Huard and halfback Rashaan Shehee in the Southern Cal game turned what could have been a top ten team into a top 25 team and instead of Pasadena it's Christmas in Honolulu.

Lettermen

Manuel Austin	Gerald Harris	Tony Parrish
Steve Bennett	Jason Harris	Jerome Pathon
Jeremy Brigham	Anthony Hicks	Jermiah Pharms
Nigel Burton	Ja'Warren Hooker	Byran Pittman
Toure Butler	Brock Huard	Mike Reed
Chris Campbell	Brad Hutt	Patrick Reddick
Andy Carroll	Joe Jarzynka	Gary Shavey
Ryan Chicoine	Jerry Jenson	Maurice Shaw
Jason Chorak	Jeff Johnson	Rashaan Shehee
Cameron Cleeland	Todd Johnson	Jermaine Smith
Tony Coats	Brendon Jones	Josh Smith
Fred Coleman	Ben Kadletz	Matt Summers
Matt Condon	Petroceli Kesi	Lester Towns
Pat Coniff	Olin Kreutz	Mac Tuiaea
Michael Coyle	Nick Lentz	MarquesTuiasosopo
Aaron Dalan	Mel Miller	Chad Ward
Dominic Daste	Anthony Mizen	John Westra
Dave Dawson	Justin Ninanabu	Sekou Wiggs
Matt Frazie	Sean O'Laughlin	
Marques Hairiston	Benji Olson	

1998

Record: 6-6-0		**Finish:** PAC-10 5th		**Coach:** Jim Lambright
Date	**UW**	**Opponent**		**Attendance**
Sept. 5	42	at Arizona St. (night)	38	72,118
Sept. 19	20	Brigham Young	10	71,297
Sept. 26	7	at Nebraska	55	76,372
Oct. 3	28	Arizona (night)	31	71,469
Oct. 10	53	Utah State	12	70,210
Oct. 17	21	California	13	71,215
Oct. 24	35	Oregon State	34	71,552
Oct. 31	10	at Southern Cal	33	62.276
Nov. 7	22	at Oregon	27	46,031
Nov. 14	24	UCLA	36	72,391
Nov. 21	16	at Washington State	9	37,251
Dec. 25	25	Air Force (Oahu Bowl)	45	46,451
Totals:	**303**		**343**	**768,976**

Co-Captains: Lester Towns, Brock Huard, Nigel Burton, Reggie Davis.

Honors

Guy Flaherty: Reggie Davis, Josh Smith. **L. Walt Rising:** Jabari Issa. **Brian Stapp:** Judd Seida. **Bob Jarvis:** Colin Beard. **All-Conference:** Jabari Issa, Joe Jarzynka.

Commentary

After defensive coach Jim Lambright was promoted to head coach, the Husky defense declined each year and in his last season Lambright's Huskies surrendered an eye-popping average of 34 points a game. As if sensing the future, Lambright said after the Washington State game, "Next year we've got to get back to basic Husky football." The sesaon could be summed up with the 60's folk song, *Blowin In the Wind:* Lambright waited one season too long to get back to basic Husky football. It was the first non-winning Husky season in 22 years.

Lettermen

Scott Ask	Todd Elstrom	Dane Looker
Manuel Austin	Matt Frazie	Omare Lowe
Colin Beard	Ryan Flemming	Anthony Mizen
Kyle Benn	Odell George	Toalei Mulitauaopele
Nigel Burton	Marques Hairiston	Roger Nelson
Toure Butler	Gerald Harris	Shawn O'Laughlin
Andy Carrol	Jason Harris	Jermaih Pharms
Braxton Cleman	Lenny Haynes	Judd Seida
Matt Condon	Ja'Warren Hooker	Jim Skurski
Kurth Connell	Brock Huard	Jermaine Smith
Pat Coniff	Brad Hutt	Josh Smith
Aaron Dalan	Joe Jarzynka	Lester Towns
Dominic Daste	Jeff Johnson	Mac Tuiaea
Wondame Davis	Brendon Jones	Marques Tuiasosopo
Dave Dawson	Ryan Julian	Chad Ward
Andre DeSessure	Ben Kadletz	Hak. Weatherspoon
Trent Dykes	Marvin Kasim	Curtis Williams
Renard Edwards	Chris Lang	

1999

Record: 7-5-0		Finish: PAC-10 2nd		Coach: Rick Neuheisel
Date	**UW**	**Opponent**		**Attendance**
Sept. 9	28	at Brigham Young (night)	35	65,726
Sept. 18	21	Air Force	31	70,019
Sept. 25	31	Colorado	24	72,068
Oct. 2	34	Oregon (night)	20	72,581
Oct. 9	47	at Oregon State	21	35,470
Oct. 16	7	Arizona State	28	72,789
Oct. 23	31	at California	27	43,000
Oct. 30	35	Stanford	30	70,308
Nov. 6	33	at Arizona	25	56.614
Nov. 13	20	at UCLA (ot)	23	55,705
Nov. 20	24	Washington State	14	72,937
Dec. 29	20	Kansas State (Holiday Bowl)	24	57,118
Totals:	**331**		**302**	**744,371**

Co-Captains: Lester Towns, Jabari Issa, Marques Tuiasosopo.

Honors

Guy Flaherty: Maurice Shaw. **L. Walt Rising:** Kurth Connell. **Brian Stapp:** Derek Noble. **Bob Jarvis:** Mathias Wilson.

Commentary

Rick Neuheisel, 42, was hired from Colorado to replace Jim Lambright. Neuheisel's first Husky team got off slowly losing their first two games and then closed strongly. The Huskies were in position to go to the Rose Bowl, but an overtime loss to UCLA in Los Angeles sent them to Holiday Bowl instead. UCLA remained a nemesis for Huskies. Season highlight was quarterback Tuiasosopo's record breaking game against Stanford.

Lettermen

Hakim Akbar	Ossim Hatem	Jeremaih Pharms
John Anderson	Lenny Haynes	Patrick Reddick
Paul Arnold	Dauan Hawkins	Sacha Sarieddine
Manuel Austin	Wilbur Hooks Jr.	J.K. Scott
Kyle Benn	Willie Hurst	Maurice Shaw
Sam Blanche	Joe Jarzynka	Geoff Shelton
Toure Butler	Ryan Julian	Elliot Silvers
Wes Call	Devon Johnson	Jim Skurski
Andy Carroll	Curt Jurgens	Jermaine Smith
Braxton Cleman	Anthony Kelley	Jerramy Stevens
Kurth Connell	Brent Knopp	Marques Tuiasosopo
Pat Coniff	Tom Larsen	Terry Tharps
Dominic Daste	Kyu Lee	Lester Towns
Darrell Daniels	Dane Looker	Larry Tripplett
Wondame Davis	Omare Lowe	Mac Tuiaea
Renard Edwards	Spencer Marona	Anthony Vonture
Todd Elstrom	Levi Madarieta	Chris Waddell
Nick Feigner	Ben Mahdavi	Chad Ward
Ryan Flemming	Ryan Miletich	Kevin Ware
Matt Fraze	Anthony Mizan	John Westra
Brian Fuller	Quinton Morgan	Curtis Williams
Odell George	Adam Marcinowski	Jafar Williams
Roderick Green	Toalei Mulitauaopele	Jamaun Willis
Marques Hairston	Rock Nelson	John Westra
Gerald Harris	Nick Olszewski	Elliot Zajac
John Hart	Rashad Petters	

2000

Record: 11-1-0		Finish: PAC-10 tie lst		Coach: Rick Neuheisel
Date	**UW**	**Opponent**		**Attendance**
Sept. 2	44	Idaho	20	70,117
Sept. 9	34	Miami (Fla.)	29	70,019
Sept. 16	17	at Colorado	14	52,068
Sept. 30	16	at Oregon	23	46,581
Oct. 7	33	Oregon State (night)	30	73,470
Oct. 14	21	at Arizona State (night)	15	61,370
Oct. 21	38	California	24	73,000
Oct. 28	31	at Stanford	28	31,300
Nov. 4	35	Arizona	32	73.614
Nov. 11	35	UCLA (night)	28	73,705
Nov. 18	51	at Washington State (night)	3	33,937
Jan. 1	34	Purdue (Rose Bowl)	24	94,392
Totals:	**389**		**270**	**747,261**

Co-Captains: Chad Ward, Elliot Silvers, Marques Tuiasosopo.

Honors

Guy Flaherty: Curtis Williams. **L. Walt Rising:** Chad Ward. **Brian Stapp:** Brian Cook, B. J. Newberry. **Bob Jarvis:** Mathias Wilson.

Commentary

If there was ever a *magical* season for the Huskies, this was it. This edition came back from a fourth quarter deficit to win no less than five times. It gave the season a feel of destiny that somehow it would end in Pasadena. It did.

Lettermen

Hakim Akbar	Odell George	Patrick Reddick
Rich Alexis	John Hart	Geoff Shelton
Roc Alexander	Ossim Hatem	Elliot Silvers
John Anderson	Lenny Haynes	J.K. Scott
Paul Arnold	Dauan Hawkins	Jim Skurski
Kyle Benn	Wilbur Hooks Jr.	Jerramy Stevens
Sam Blanche	Willie Hurst	Terry Tharps
Toure Butler	Derrick Johnson	MarquesTuiasosopo
Wes Call	Ryan Julian	Larry Tripplett
Gregg Carothers	Curt Jurgens	Anthony Vonture
Braxton Cleman	Anthony Kelley	Chris Waddell
Joe Collier	Brent Knopp	Chad Ward
Pat Coniff	Omare Lowe	Kevin Ware
Dominic Daste	Spencer Marona	John Westra
Darrell Daniels	Levi Madarieta	Curtis Williams
Wondame Davis	Ben Mahdavi	Jafar Williams
Todd Elstrom	Rock Nelson	Jamaun Willis
Ryan Flemming	Nick Olszewski	John Westra
Matt Fraze	Jeremaih Pharms	Elliot Zajac

INDEX

Photo Credits

Page 7, Jim Owens and team, Seattle P-I & MOHAI.*

Page 104, Rick Redman, Univ. of Washington.

Page 106, Al Worley, Univ. of Washington.

Page 109, Koll Hagen, Univ. of Washington.

Page 111, Rudy Reuttiger & Rick Neuheisel, Roger Burke.

Page 119, Larry Clanton, Clanton Estate.

Page 123, Ray Mansfield, Roy McKasson, John Meyers, Univ. of Washington.

Page 126, John F. Kennedy, Seattle P-I & MOHAI.

Page 132, Koll Hagen, Univ. of Washinton. Koll Hagen, Roger Burke.

*Seattle Museum of History and Industry.